Doctoral De-Stress

How to Thrive on Your PhD Journey

Dr Serena K Sharma

To request permissions, contact the author at
info@academease.org

ISBN (paperback): 978-1-8381816-0-4
ISBN (e-book): 978-1-8381816-1-1

Cover photo by MD Duran on Unsplash

Published by Folly Bridge Press
Oxford, United Kingdom

Visit the *AcademEase* website at
www.academease.org

For my mother, Asha Parashar-Reynolds

CONTENTS

ACKNOWLEDGMENTS

This book would not have been possible without three very special people.

Chris, thank you for enthusiastically supporting me with this project from start to finish. You were instrumental in helping me to set up *AcademEase* and have continued to cheer me on every step of the way. I wouldn't have been able to complete this book without you.

Oliver, I wrote every word of this book while you were peacefully sleeping beside me. I am grateful to you for every spare moment that you allowed me to write. I am also grateful to you for the nights that you wouldn't sleep, as it prompted me to make the most of the time that I did have!

Mom, this book is dedicated to you because you introduced me to world of wellness from a very young age. I used to tease you about your taste in books and now I find myself drawn to the exact same ones. I've learned so much from you and am glad that we have this passion in common. Thank you for everything.

INTRODUCTION:
YOUR PHD DOESN'T HAVE TO BE
A STRUGGLE

It was a brisk autumn day in 2015 and I was about to start a new job at the London School of Economics. As I walked into the main building to get my academic staff card, the security guard asked me for my name and then typed it into his computer. He then looked back at me with a confused expression: 'that's strange, we already have an ID card registered to someone with your name on our system.' I explained to him that the person on the system was in fact me. Over a decade earlier I had been enrolled at LSE as a PhD student.

The security guard let out a chuckle and then smiled at me warmly. 'Alright Dr Sharma, it appears you've come full circle. Welcome home.' In many ways I did feel like I was coming home, back to the place where my journey as a PhD student began. 'Since we already have a photo of you on the system...' he began to ask, 'shall we just use the one we have or would you like a new photo taken?' Given that the existing photo was now over a decade old, I figured it might be a good idea to get an updated one, so I quickly had a new photo taken. I must have left in a hurry because I didn't realise that the security guard had mistakenly issued my staff card with the older photo. This would later turn out to be a very serendipitous mistake.

After going back to my office and discovering that I had been given a staff card with the wrong photo, I began to study that decade-old-photo of myself. Apart from briefly lamenting how quickly the time had passed, I started to think back to the person I was when that photo was taken, the person who first embarked on a PhD all those years ago.

As I looked into the eyes of past me, the first thing I noticed was how terrified she appeared. Although she had dreamt about studying at LSE, making that dream a reality meant moving to a foreign country and leaving her loved ones behind. I felt a lot of compassion for that younger version of myself. I wished there was some way I could go back and tell her that things were going to be OK and that she'd make it through her PhD. It would have been reassuring to hear that, especially on the days that didn't feel OK. The days that were filled with stress, self-doubt and loneliness, when I wondered if I was ever going to finish and if it would even be worth all the struggle.

The process of completing a PhD is quite unlike any other undertaking. It's a huge investment of time, energy and money. With most doctoral theses ranging between 80,000 to 100,000 words, it is an understatement to say that the process demands a high degree of self-discipline, commitment and sacrifice. For many students, it can feel like an exceptionally long and bumpy road, with many ups and downs along the way.

The more onerous features of PhD life are of course balanced out by the many benefits of completing a doctorate. Apart from the potential to set you off on a different career path and open up doors, having a doctorate in hand can also feel deeply satisfying. Whether it's the start of a larger body of research or an end in itself, a doctorate represents your own unique contribution to a particular field. The topics that students choose to research are often deeply personal for them, which brings further meaning to the pursuit of a PhD.

Within the world of academia there are few things

that feel as rewarding as completing a doctorate. Yet, there still tends to be a lot of mystery surrounding the PhD process. It's not comparable to any other degree in academia – nor is it comparable to any job. Despite having supervisors and pastoral support available, there is actually very little guidance on how to make it through the process in one piece.

When I reflect on my own PhD experience, what strikes me is how much stress I endured throughout. I firmly believed that the stress I felt was an inevitable part of being a PhD student. My perception was shaped by a number of formative experiences and solidified by the people I encountered on my path.

One particularly strong memory that stands out is a panel discussion I attended during my first week in the doctoral programme. The panel consisted of second- and third-year PhD students and was intended to be an opportunity to learn about what to expect in the first year. When it came to the Q&A portion of the discussion, one of my peers asked a panellist if he had any tips for managing stress and I'll never forget his response. He said 'you're a PhD student; you're meant to be stressed out.'

While everyone chuckled at what seemed to be a light-hearted, throwaway comment, what it does reflect is a particular attitude towards stress in higher education. It's a view that is outdated and even dangerous when considering the ongoing mental health crisis across universities today.[1] To tacitly accept PhD stress as inevitable does an immense disservice to students. Nevertheless, the words of that panellist 'you're a PhD student; you're meant to be stressed out' were etched into my mind. This became the mantra I would live by during the years I spent as a doctoral student. Not surprisingly, it made my PhD experience much more of a struggle than it needed to be.

As I kept staring at that old photo of myself, I started to feel a sense of purpose. I couldn't go back and help that younger version of me, but what if I could help other students? What if I could let them know that pursuing a doctorate didn't need to be a struggle? This strong desire planted a seed in my mind that eventually led me to become involved in student wellness. It was shortly thereafter that I launched a series of wellness workshops, which were tailored to the unique stresses that PhD students face. I also began coaching doctoral students in small groups as well as one-to-one. What started off as a hobby blossomed into *AcademEase*,[2] an organisation dedicated to helping students navigate academic stress. Through *AcademEase*, I was brought into contact with university staff and students across several universities.

Having the opportunity to contribute to PhD student wellness has been one of the most rewarding experiences of my career. When I reflect on how it all came about, I feel a deep sense of gratitude for the security guard that gave me the wrong ID card. Had I not been forced to reflect on my own PhD experience by looking at that old photo of myself, I might never have been spurred into action.

After working with hundreds of PhD students across multiple institutions, I have been amazed by how much they have in common. Despite the variation in their research projects, not to mention their different disciplinary backgrounds, the types of challenges they face are remarkably similar. *Doctoral De-Stress: How to Thrive on Your PhD Journey* features the top 40 challenges that doctoral students face, in their own words, while offering tips and advice for navigating each one. It is a compilation of all the things I wish I had known when I started my PhD and everything I would go back and tell that younger version of myself if I had the chance.

- The first chapter, 'Enter the Inner Critic', explores that internal voice which tells us we aren't good enough to be doing a PhD in the first place.

- The second chapter, 'Writing Woes', surveys the many writing-related challenges that come up for PhD students, from perfectionism and procrastination to writer's block.

- Chapter Three, 'Persisting with the PhD', offers techniques for sustaining motivation and reconnecting to what first inspired you to pursue a doctorate.

- Perhaps the most fundamental relationship we have throughout a PhD is the one with our academic supervisors. Chapter Four, 'Supervisor Stress', examines some of the challenges that may arise in that relationship and how to overcome them.

- Chapter Five, 'Roadblocks and Detours on the PhD Path', considers how to manage any unexpected issues that surface during doctoral study.

- Chapter Six, 'Putting Your Ideas (and Yourself) Out There', puts forward a set of tips for presenting academic work and sharing your ideas more broadly.

- Chapter Seven, 'Juggling the PhD With Other Commitments', discusses ways to balance the competing priorities on your PhD plate.

- The eighth and final chapter, 'Defending Your Work: Navigating the Viva Process', delves into the viva examination and the key steps involved in preparing for it.

Pursuing a PhD really doesn't have to be a struggle. The practical advice, expert tips and heartfelt support offered in this book will empower you to thrive during your doctorate. *Doctoral De-Stress* can either be read cover-to-cover, or used as a reference guide in response to specific challenges as they arise. You will also find a number of book bonuses available as supplementary material on the *AcademEase* website (www.academease.org).

To all of the students who have found their way to this book, it is my sincere hope that *Doctoral De-Stress* will become an invaluable companion to you throughout your PhD journey.

1

ENTER THE INNER CRITIC

I don't belong in a PhD programme

I've worked with my fair share of bright, talented and hardworking PhD students over the years. While their backgrounds and projects may have varied considerably, there was one factor that every single one of them had in common – none of them felt they were actually good enough to be doing a PhD! These students were crippled with a form of self-doubt that I believe is very much endemic to completing a doctorate.

A PhD is the highest degree awarded in academia, so it's no wonder that doctoral students experience a significant level of self-doubt as they embark on this journey. What I found to be quite striking were the range of stories they told me – and most importantly themselves – about how ill-prepared they were for the task ahead.

Whether it was because they had crossed over from another discipline, or perhaps they had switched to the PhD from an entirely different field altogether. Or it could have simply been a consequence of the unfamiliar ground they were treading in their theses which made them feel out of their depth. Whatever the circumstances, these students had managed to convince themselves that they didn't belong in a PhD programme. Their aim was to simply scrape through and hope no one would take notice of the fact that they didn't actually belong.

After hearing these stories time and time again, I noticed that what so many students were suffering from is an academic version of Imposter Syndrome. According to the Harvard Business Review, Imposter Syndrome can be defined as 'a collection of feelings of inadequacy that persist despite evident success.'[3] The interesting thing about Imposter Syndrome is that it affects people in all walks of life irrespective – or perhaps owing to – their levels of success. In her recently published autobiography, Michelle Obama acknowledged her own struggles with Imposter Syndrome.[4]

While Imposter Syndrome can affect just about anybody, I believe it has particular purchase in university settings and that PhD students are especially prone. In fact, I have yet to come across a single PhD student who hasn't experienced some element of 'Academic Imposter Syndrome' throughout their PhD journey.

There are several aspects of a PhD that make doctoral students likely candidates for Imposter Syndrome. First and foremost, academia is by its very nature a competitive domain that tends to attract high achievers. A doctoral thesis sets out to make a significant contribution towards the furtherance of knowledge in a specific area, with each student expected to write as an authority on his or her subject. In this sense, a PhD student commences their doctoral journey with something to prove to others and to themselves.

While this can amount to a significant degree of pressure on one's shoulders, this pressure is compounded by the reality that PhD theses are independent projects. Despite having a supervisor (or supervisors in certain cases), most doctoral students are offered very little guidance on the process of completing their doctorates, what benchmarks they are required to meet throughout or how to even start. A student once described the process as being thrown in at the deep end where their only options are to sink or swim. It is no wonder that so many students find themselves swimming against the tide of self-doubt and yielding to the Imposter persona.

For many, the voice of the imposter ends up permeating all aspects of the PhD. It facilitates an unwinnable comparison between themselves and others, with the perpetual feeling that everyone else is performing much better. It leads students to question whether or not they will ever be able to finish their projects. And even when the end is in sight, this lingering voice has each student doubt if their work is actually good enough. In short, Academic Imposter Syndrome sucks the joy away from the PhD process and makes the journey of obtaining a doctorate much more exhausting than it needs to be. In the following sections, I will examine the voice of the Imposter in more depth.

All of my colleagues are further ahead than me

Among the countless factors that tend to fuel the voice

of the Imposter, perhaps none is as powerful as comparing ourselves to others. The comparison game can seem like a perfectly benign exercise yet it is so often to our detriment. I can't count the number of students who told me they felt like things were proceeding perfectly well with their work until they found out how their peers were doing.

In many ways, the competitive nature of academia encourages us to compare ourselves to others. With our work being constantly assessed and evaluated, measuring our progress in relation to others can start to feel very natural. Moreover, trying to get a sense of how others are performing can seem a useful way for determining how well we are doing. At the same time, there is also something deeply counterproductive about assessing our progress on the PhD in relation to others. This became particularly evident to me when I was completing my own doctorate.

At the PhD level, there is no obvious basis for comparison between each student. Although doctoral students tend to have some course work during their first year and yearly upgrade panels, these don't tend to be graded. Each student pursues their own independent research projects over a three or four-year period (longer in some places) wherein the only requirement is to submit an 80,000-10,0000-word thesis.

What I noticed when I was completing my PhD was how – given that our main task was to write a thesis – the default mode of comparison became how many chapters each of us had produced. I recall being asked several times throughout my PhD by other classmates: 'how many chapters have you written?' and feeling bad that it wasn't enough in comparison to what some of the other students had managed to produce. It started to feed into the feeling that I was behind and not performing as well as my colleagues. This in turn magnified my own sense of being an imposter.

What the chapter counting took no notice of was how unique each PhD project was, not to mention the distinct working patterns of each student, differences in their methodology, and the resulting variations in terms of the timescales for completion. Given all of this, counting chapters as a measure for comparison – and draft chapters in particular – was pretty meaningless.

The futility of this metric became even more apparent as the time for submitting the thesis drew nearer. Interestingly, and to my surprise, those who had written the most in the initial stages of the PhD were by no means the first to submit. This really brought home to me how ridiculous the chapter counting comparison was. But my realization also applies to the more general comparisons we tend to draw between ourselves and others. Whether we are using academic benchmarks or another metric for comparison, we will always find people who seem to be doing better than us, as well as people who may not be – it all depends on where we focus our attention.

Either way, we'd be much better off not to make the success, failure, progress or lack of progress of others mean something about ourselves. No two PhDs are alike and, therefore, it really is pointless to assess your PhD progress in relation to others.

Will I ever finish?

At one point or another, every PhD student asks themselves if they will ever actually finish their thesis. The trek up the PhD mountain can seem insurmountable and there are several reasons for this.

For one, the work involved in completing a thesis can seem endless. Once you finish one chapter or paper, there are inevitably more to do. It's natural to wonder if you'll ever get to the end when there always seems to be more work hiding around the next corner.

The doubts relating to whether or not you'll finish also have a lot to do with the uncertainty surrounding research. Since most PhD theses set out to analyse or answer a specific question, it is highly likely that you won't be sure about your conclusions until you actually reach the point of concluding your work. Without knowing how you will get to that point or what your thesis will end up arguing, you have to somehow trust that the path will unfold as you walk along it. This takes a great leap of faith.

I believe that the focus on finishing is symptomatic of an outcome-oriented mindset that is prevalent among most PhD students. In accordance with this mindset, a PhD tends to be defined by its end product – the submission of a thesis. Although this may be a true account of what a doctorate entails, it does not accurately reflect the actual experience of producing a PhD.

For most students, completing a PhD is not a straightforward or direct path. In actuality, it is based on a series of uneven steps, and even missteps, that by their very nature proceed in fits and starts. In fact, it is not uncommon for a student to find that they have little to show for entire days, weeks and perhaps even months of work. This is all part of the process of completing a PhD. It is precisely for this reason that I prefer to consider the PhD as a process – not an outcome.

A process-oriented approach takes some of the pressure off by shifting away from the outcome and allowing students to focus on the day-to-day tasks that will lead to that much desired end point.

How can we adopt a more process-oriented mindset when it comes to pursuing a PhD?

The main tool that I've found to be quite useful is what I refer to as a PhD Process Journal. At the end of your work day, spend a few moments writing out what you did that day. Do this not as a way to judge yourself for having done too little, but specifically to remind yourself of the nature of the project. A thesis cannot be completed in one day, but only in a series of smaller steps.

This simple tool enables you to feel forward movement, even on days when you might be stuck and are going in circles. A journaling technique, such as this, provides a constant reminder that setbacks are just a part of the process. What this does is build up some positive momentum and allows you to recognize that you are on your way irrespective of how close (or far!) you may feel you are to finishing.

What if my work isn't good enough?

The expectations associated with a PhD thesis are not just high, oftentimes they are unrealistically high. Many students have the impression that their thesis must be a brilliant piece of work that will define who they are and what they will do for years to come. Consequently, even when the finish line is in sight, another concern swiftly arises – will the end product be good enough?

Given that so many PhD students tend to define themselves in relation to their work, the question of 'is this good enough?' quickly becomes 'am I good enough?'

While the bar may seem exceptionally high when it comes to producing a doctoral thesis, the reality is that the standard is a lot lower than one might expect. My doctoral supervisor used to refer to the PhD as an apprenticeship. This seems to be a more realistic description of what the process entails and what is expected in terms of the output.

If you were to take a look at some of the PhD theses in your university library that are within your field, you may be surprised at what you find. What you will likely observe is that these projects are not masterpieces that completely break new ground. In stark contrast to being overly ambitious, the purpose of a PhD thesis is to answer a single question or problem within a set of clearly defined parameters. In this regard, a PhD thesis tends to open up as many questions as answers and, as such, need not be thought of as your life's work.

A further thing to bear in mind whenever you start to worry about the quality of your thesis and whether it is 'good enough' is the way in which it will be evaluated. Unlike other pieces of work that you have produced in your academic career, all you need to do is pass. Recalling that the thesis will not be graded in the traditional sense may help to alleviate some of the concerns surrounding whether it is good enough.

I'll feel more confident when I've submitted

So far, we've explored the voice of the Academic Imposter in terms of the tendency to compare ourselves to others, the concerns relating to finishing and finally, doubts surrounding whether the end product will be good enough. As is evident, the process of completing a doctorate is one that is riddled with self-doubt.

If the PhD is associated with such significant levels of self-doubt, the clearest antidote to this is to finish. Many students expect that when they submit their doctoral thesis, the self-doubt will automatically lift and that will allow them to step into greater confidence. I certainly thought this would be the case when I submitted. In order to understand why this is not the case, it is important to reflect a bit more, and also reframe the phenomenon of the Imposter.

To a certain extent I believe we are all afflicted by some version of Imposter Syndrome, but I tend to think of it slightly differently. Rather than perceiving this extreme form of self-doubt in terms of a 'syndrome', I prefer to reframe it as a disowned part of myself, a part that I call the Inner Critic. By reframing it in this way, it allows me to take ownership of this part of myself and puts me in a better position to not only work with, but also make peace with it.

The thing that's so interesting about the Inner Critic is that it does not get any quieter as we achieve more. In fact, the more that we experience success, the louder it tends to get. I found this out the hard way when I finally submitted my thesis. I kept telling myself that I would start to feel confident when I could call myself a doctor, but I actually just felt more insecure as I experienced the pressures of post-PhD life – applying for jobs, trying to publish my first book, giving my first lecture. It was all very new to me and way out of my comfort zone. Suddenly I had graduated from being a student and was now among peers in a much bigger pond, with seemingly much more at stake. As soon as I came to this realisation, my inner critic started to chatter: 'What makes you think you are good enough to be here?'; 'Why aren't you working harder?'; 'Everyone has published their first book by now'; 'You won't have enough funding to extend your post'; 'You aren't good enough to be an academic.'

The most common approach to dealing with the ramblings of the Inner Critic is to ignore it. If we don't engage with these statements they will eventually go away, right? Unfortunately, this is usually not the case. If achieving higher levels of success is not enough to quiet down the Inner Critic, covering our ears and running from it won't do it either.

From my experience, the best way to turn down the volume on the Inner Critic is to actually listen to what it has to say. This will involve following a series of steps, which I have included as an exercise in the *Doctoral De-Stress* Book Bonuses page 'Turning Down the Volume on Your Inner Critic' on academease.org.

Chapter One Takeaways

☐ There are several aspects of a PhD that make doctoral students likely candidates for Academic Imposter Syndrome. Not only does Academic Imposter Syndrome remove the joy from the PhD process, it makes the journey of obtaining a doctorate much more exhausting than it needs to be.

☐ Whether we are using academic benchmarks or another metric for comparison, we will always find people who seem to be doing better than us, as well as people who may not be – it all depends on where we focus our attention. Either way, we'd be much better off not to make the success, failure, progress or lack of progress of others mean something about ourselves. No two PhDs are alike and, therefore, it is pointless to assess your PhD progress in relation to others.

☐ Try viewing the PhD as a process rather than an outcome. A process-oriented approach takes some of the pressure off by moving away from the outcome and allowing students to focus on the day-to-day tasks that will lead to their desired end point. A PhD Process Journal can help to shift towards a process-oriented mindset.

☐ A PhD thesis tends to open up as many questions as answers and, as such, need not be thought of as your life's work.

☐ The best way to turn down the volume on your Inner Critic is to actually listen to what it has to say. For further guidance on how to do this, see the *Doctoral De-Stress* Book Bonuses on academease.org.

2

WRITING WOES

I have writer's block

While PhD requirements tend to vary by discipline, the one thing that every doctoral student will be expected to do a lot of is write. Whether we like it or not, writing is an essential part of producing a doctoral thesis. Whereas some find the 'writing up' phase to be one of the most straightforward aspects of their PhD, others find the writing process to be extremely cumbersome.

There are several aspects of academic writing that students tend to find challenging. Academic writing is often regarded as being unnecessarily complex, excessively lengthy, and overly reliant on footnotes. There is also the constant worry of how the writing will be received and evaluated. With one half of you perpetually questioning whether your supervisor will like what you are writing, it can be exceptionally difficult to stay present enough to actually get any writing done!

What can be particularly frustrating are those occasions when you have a perfectly clear plan or outline in your mind, but are somehow unable to translate that plan into writing. You may sit in front of your computer for hours or days on end, with little to show for that time. Evidently writer's block doesn't just occur to those pursuing creative writing endeavours.

When it comes to strategies for overcoming writer's block, there are a variety of different approaches one can take. At one end of the spectrum is the 'Dive In' approach. Rather than waiting for the block to lift, the idea behind this approach is to simply dive in and begin writing – because sometimes the simple act of writing is enough to help remove a block. This can take the form of 'pre-writing', where you dedicate some time before you begin working to write down all of your unedited thoughts; a brainstorming session, where you write down key words or phrases relating to your specific project; or a simple free writing exercise, where you set a timer and write down whatever comes to you.

The reason why the Dive In approach works is because it limits the time available for worry and overthinking (for those who may be susceptible to either). Instead, it approaches the writing process as a muscle that functions best when it's exercised regularly. It allows for the fact that writing is a more dynamic exercise than we give it credit for. For example, we are still thinking and formulating ideas as we write, which is why even the most meticulously planned outline will look very different when it's been written out. When we simply dive in, we allow for that dynamic process to take shape.

An alternative approach to overcoming writer's block

is to step back from the writing altogether. While it's commonly believed that we have to power through a case of writer's block to overcome it, the reality is that the block may be caused by undue proximity to our work. When we are too close to our writing, it can lead to myopia, such that we may not be able to see a way through a problem. In such cases, getting some distance may be the only way to get unstuck. I know from my own experience that when I've been stuck on a particular piece of writing, the solution tends to comes to me when I'm not actively thinking about it, but doing something unrelated.

Whichever strategy we might use to get unstuck, the thing about writer's block is that it tends to be a symptom of something much deeper. In the case of a PhD student, writer's block tends to mask the fears associated with producing a thesis. After all, the expectations surrounding a doctoral degree are high and the pressure on students is understandably immense. We want the project to reflect our best work and to make a significant contribution to knowledge in our chosen field. The fear that our work may not match this high standard is, I believe, one of the clearest explanations for why doctoral students experience writer's block.

The menace of striving for PhD perfection has a number of knock-on effects for students. For one, it may unwittingly encourage students to be unrealistic in terms of what they aim to cover in their projects. With limited time and scope to produce a thesis, attempting to cover too much ground can easily lead a project to expand beyond its scope and go off track. The ambition to produce a perfect piece of work may also manifest in a rather different tendency and that is the avoidance of work altogether, becoming distracted by anything and everything apart from the thesis. In this way, perfectionism may show up as procrastination.

As is evident, PhD writer's block is a multi-faceted issue. The sections that follow will explore the causes and consequences of writer's block in more depth, as well as tips for getting unstuck.

I'm struggling with perfectionism

With the constant pressure to achieve in academia it is no surprise that perfectionism is so prevalent among students. The consequences of perfectionism can be quite debilitating, as a recent study published in the journal *Personality and Individual Differences* reveals a correlation between perfectionism and depression.[5]

While the causes may vary from case to case, more often than not, perfectionism stems from a fear of making mistakes. I've noticed this particularly among PhD students who approach prospective mistakes as unequivocal proof that they don't belong or are not good enough to pursue a PhD. Determined not to let this happen, many students obsess over every detail of their PhDs and may even find excuses to hold off on sharing drafts of their thesis.

When it comes to managing perfectionism, the words we use to describe our work can carry a lot of weight. For instance, whenever I tell myself that I'm in the process of writing a 'chapter', I instantly feel the weight of what I'm working on and the expectations surrounding it. *Who is going to read it? What if it isn't any good? Why am I bothering with this in the first place?* This is how I talk myself out of doing things before I've even started.

To mitigate this, I try and soften the language I use

surrounding the task. Whether it's a lecture I'm preparing or a chapter I'm writing, I almost always refer to it as a 'sketch', 'outline' or even a 'blueprint', and I preface whatever I produce as 'preliminary.' While it can feel heavy to expect myself to produce a full article, writing a preliminary sketch is something I can do.

With this very subtle shift in language, I immediately alleviate any pressure and anxiety associated with the task. It's a way of tricking my mind into relaxing while I move closer to completing my work. In this way, the task I would otherwise endlessly worry about gets completed without me really noticing it.

In addition to shifting our language in order to defuse the pressures associated with producing a thesis, it can also be helpful to shift our expectations of the PhD itself. On that note, the next time you find yourself crippled by perfectionism, try to bear in mind the following points:

1. **It's Not Your Life's Work:** Given the dedication and time it takes to complete a doctoral thesis, it is not uncommon to feel as though the end result must amount to your life's work. However, this could not be further from the truth. In stark contrast to being overly ambitious, the purpose of a PhD thesis is to answer a single question or problem within a set of clearly defined parameters. In this regard, a PhD thesis tends to open up as many questions as it answers.

2. **It's a Pass/Fail:** Unlike other degrees in academia, the PhD viva is a straightforward pass or fail. While that may sound daunting, the fact is that all you need to do is obtain a passing mark and no amount of going above and beyond the requirements will change that. As the end product will not be graded

in the traditional sense, it is worth considering whether you might already have enough material on hand to pass the viva.

3. **It's Never Really 'Done':** As unsatisfying as it may seem, the truth about academic research is that it's never really done. Any piece of research should be viewed as a general snapshot at a specific moment in time. For instance, take a look at something that was published quite recently (this year or even this month) which you consider to be a strong piece of work. Irrespective of how strong a piece it is, you can probably identify areas in which that piece could be updated, improved, or revised in line with recent developments. By its very nature, academic research is dynamic and continuously evolving.

4. **You'll (Most Likely) End up Revising It Anyways:** Although most students feel under pressure to produce a flawless piece of work, the truth is that PhD theses are rarely, if ever, published as they are. For instance, when it comes to publishing, students are often expected to revise their theses prior to submitting it to a journal or an academic press. This is the case whether the PhD consists of a larger book-style manuscript or a series of separate papers. The likely need for some form of revision or updating if you intend to publish your thesis will hopefully lessen some of the pressures associated with producing a perfect end product.

As the above points demonstrate, shifting our expectations of the PhD can go a long way towards overcoming perfectionism. When we have a more realistic picture of what the PhD entails, we can start to let go of the fear of making mistakes and perhaps even embrace the inevitable imperfections in our work. Your PhD is not going to be perfect, and the good news is that it doesn't need to be.

I have too many ideas to fit in my thesis

When we think of a PhD student plagued by writer's block, we might have an image of a student staring at a blank page, struggling to come up with a sufficient number of words. The real challenge in writing up a doctoral thesis is not, however, in having too little to say, but too much. It is not uncommon for students to find themselves stuck over what to exclude in the final version of their thesis.

The further you get into your PhD project, the more likely it is that your research will spark new ideas. This is a natural and exhilarating aspect of pursuing doctoral research. The more you explore one path, other paths of interest begin to open up. What becomes difficult is trying to incorporate all of these new ideas and areas of interest into a project that is by its very nature limited — not just in terms of the words you have to work with and the time you have available, but also the scope of the project. New ideas can often expand the parameters of the PhD to something that becomes overly ambitious, unmanageable, and far beyond what would be reasonable for a single thesis to accommodate.

The reality of being unable to incorporate all of your great ideas into the thesis might become a recipe for dissatisfaction with the final product. When this occurs, it is important to find a way to accept that you simply won't have the space to say and do everything that you find interesting on your topic. Equally, it is important to have a designated space to record whatever insights flood your mind throughout your PhD research.

My recommendation to help balance this inevitable wave of creativity on the one hand, with the limits of your project on the other, is to invest in an Ideas Journal. An Ideas Journal is a notebook for the sole purpose of storing pieces of inspiration, random thoughts, and creative insights that may be related to your PhD project, but not specifically intended for inclusion in the thesis itself. There are numerous benefits to investing in an Ideas Journal.

First of all, an Ideas Journal can accommodate anything of interest to you on your topic that doesn't necessarily fit within the confines of your project. By alleviating the pressure to incorporate everything within your thesis, it can help mitigate the risk of your project going off course. As you utilise the journal, you simultaneously reaffirm the boundaries of your research and in so doing, cultivate the necessary focus to complete your PhD.

Second, having a record of ideas that are related to your PhD, but not at the core of your project, can easily be fed into the concluding chapter of your thesis under the 'areas for further research' section. Highlighting avenues for further research is an important component of a doctoral thesis, as it allows you to highlight where your work is situated within the broader field and to identify what potential avenues for research it opens up. Having some insights into how future research could build on your specific project will also give you something to discuss with your viva examiners.

Third, it can be a place to brainstorm your plans after the PhD. This can either be some ideas for how you might like to revise your thesis for publication, or alternatively, it could be a few notes which form the basis of a post-doctoral project. Using an Ideas Journal to flesh out prospective post-PhD projects serves as a powerful reminder that there is life beyond your current project. This will go a long way towards helping you escape the type of tunnel vision that is sometimes endemic to the PhD experience.

Finally, even if you don't have waves of inspiration or insights that might automatically be included in your Ideas Journal, it may still serve a very useful purpose. As you get further into defining your research question, you'll likely realize what is possible and what isn't within the parameters of your PhD project. This will typically result in some element of downsizing. While it can be tough to scale back on your original plans, especially if it involves cutting out earlier material that you've spent a lot of time on, having a safe space to store this material can make the task of letting it go much more palatable.

Whichever way you decide to utilise your Ideas Journal, you'll find it to be an immensely powerful tool, not simply for maintaining focus and exercising creativity, but also in terms of tapping into that sense of excitement surrounding your broader subject area. This will undoubtedly serve you well, particularly during the long, and sometimes arduous, writing-up phase.

How can I stop procrastinating?

I have yet to come across a PhD student who hasn't struggled at some point with procrastination. When faced with a task as momentous as writing a thesis, almost any other activity can appear more appealing. This makes it very easy to give in to distractions.

The distraction may be an administrative task or

chores that feel lighter than the PhD and are by nature easier to tick off our 'to-do' list. For instance, if you've reached a challenging juncture in your research, doing the dishes or laundry probably feels like a welcome escape. Your preferred method of procrastination may also take the form of social media, Netflix, or an interesting hobby.

A further set of distractions could involve work related to the PhD, that trick us into feeling like we are progressing with our work while simultaneously avoiding what we are meant to be working on. A good example of this is continuing to read new literature on our topic, when we are meant to be cracking on with writing. This is an especially popular mode of distraction for PhD students given the amount of literature available and the related expectation to be 'experts' in our respective fields. We can so easily fool ourselves into thinking we need to keep on reading. Yet, the real reason that so many students read to their heart's content, and in turn delay their writing, is because it may feel safer to read someone else's work than to start writing your own.

I must admit that I've engaged in all of the above modes of procrastination throughout my PhD. The moments when I seemed particularly prone to distraction were ironically those days that I had the most time available. For instance, after blocking out an entire day in the expectation of getting some serious writing done, for whatever reason I would find that I had very little to show for that particular day. Reflecting on this experience has highlighted to me the importance of managing my time as a way to better manage my tendency to procrastinate. In order to do this, I've come to rely upon a tool that enables me to set some parameters around my time.

The first step is to identify a task that you'd like to complete. It could simply be the next section of your thesis that you'd like to write, responding to an email, or another item on your to-do list. Next, set a timer for 25 minutes and for this period of time, do nothing but the task you have identified. After 25 minutes take a short break and then get ready to do another 25-minute round. This simple practice is called the Pomodoro Technique, developed by Francesco Cirillo.[6]

Having used this tool quite a lot I can definitely attest that it works. There's something about breaking tasks down into manageable increments and setting boundaries around your time that helps to manage distractions. I've found that once I carve out the time and space to complete a task through this technique, it becomes a lot easier to protect that time from things that might otherwise encroach on it.

For instance, if the phone rings while I'm in the middle of a Pomodoro round, I'll let it go to voicemail; if I feel tempted to go on social media or check my email, I'll simply wait. The technique works just as well for short-term tasks as it does for longer-term projects. And since mobile phones are often the biggest distraction for many of us, I usually begin this practice by putting my phone on airline mode.

I keep missing my writing deadlines

There is no denying that doctoral students enjoy a great deal of freedom. Although they have a supervisor, most PhD students pursue their work independently. No one tends to monitor their research on a daily basis and it is largely up to them to decide how to use their time.

One of the consequences of working independently is

that students are usually free to set their own deadlines. Nevertheless, despite having complete control over their schedules, I've observed so many students struggling to meet their writing deadlines. This is ironic given that, as noted above, the deadlines are most likely determined by students themselves. So how does this happen?

Having been in this position a lot myself as a student, and continuing to observe it among the students I've worked with, I've realised that the inability to meet writing deadlines is not simply a coincidence or a shared trait of all PhD students. In my view, the frequency of missing deadlines derives from a crucial misconception surrounding the writing process that has a direct bearing on how we plan. Let's explore this further.

Whenever I have a deadline approaching, I usually spend a bit of time planning how long a piece of writing will take and how much time I will need to devote to it each day. For instance, if I was aiming to complete a 10,000-word chapter, I might set a goal of writing 1,000 words per day over the course of 10 days. This is the approach I had consistently taken throughout my PhD and, at first glance, it does seem perfectly reasonable. There was, however, something very crucial that I had been overlooking in my planning process, or to be more specific, an incorrect assumption that I was making.

I assumed not only that every day that I worked on that task would be the same, but also that it *should* be the same. After years and years of doing this, I came to see that this could not be further from the truth. What I encountered in reality was a much greater degree of variance between each day that I spent working on a task. There were days when things just flowed and I ended up exceeding what I had hoped to accomplish in that day. Then there were the days that I struggled to make any progress whatsoever. Sometimes the progress I made during the exceptionally good days would even out my lack of progress on the 'off days', and I would still hit my targeted deadline. Other times I was forced to go back to my initial schedule and amend my completion date. This never felt particularly good.

Despite knowing that my instinctual approach to planning doesn't work, I still sometimes feel drawn to plan in this way. What this demonstrates is a reluctance to acknowledge that ebb days are inevitable. Acknowledging this would not only lead to a messier schedule, it would also feel like I was somehow inviting more of those days in, which I definitely did not want.

After a lot of reflection, I've come to see the value in taking a more flexible approach to planning, by building in time for less productive days and unexpected delays. In other words, allowing for both the ebbs and flows that are part of the writing process. Now, on the days when I accomplish less than I would have hoped, I try not to make it a big deal. I can see that what I used to perceive as a 'bad day' was not really a bad day at all – it was simply an outcome of the fact that no two days of writing will be exactly the same.

In short, when it comes to writing, our instincts are almost always to overcommit and underdeliver. This means, aiming for peak productivity (promising more than may be possible), which results in under delivering (failing to achieve your desired results). Rather than following this unruly pattern, the next time you have writing deadline, try the reverse – under-committing and overdelivering.

Chapter Two Takeaways

☐ The expectations surrounding a doctoral degree are high and the pressure on students is understandably immense. We want the project to reflect our best work and to make a significant contribution to knowledge in our chosen field. The fear that our work may not match this high standard is one of the clearest explanations for why doctoral students experience writer's block.

☐ When it comes to managing perfectionism, the words we use to describe our work can carry a lot of weight. Try and soften the language you use around the task (using words such as 'preliminary', 'sketch' or 'blueprint'). With this very subtle shift in language, you can trick your mind into relaxing while moving closer to completion.

☐ An Ideas Journal is a notebook for the sole purpose of storing pieces of inspiration, random thoughts and creative insights that may be related to your PhD project, but not specifically intended for inclusion in the thesis itself. As you utilise the journal, you simultaneously reaffirm the boundaries of your research.

☐ The next time you find yourself distracted, try the Pomodoro Technique. Breaking tasks down into manageable increments and setting boundaries around your time helps to cultivate focus.

☐ When it comes to setting writing deadlines, it is natural to overcommit and underdeliver. This means aiming for peak productivity (promising more than may be possible), which results in underdelivering (failing to achieve your desired results). Rather than following this pattern, try the opposite – under-committing and overdelivering.

3

PERSISTING WITH THE PHD:
THE CHALLENGE OF STAYING
MOTIVATED

I feel unmotivated

With PhD projects averaging around 4 or more years to complete, it can be difficult to sustain the motivation that inspired you to start the project in the first place. A lack of motivation can show up in many different ways. Whether it's procrastination, feeling low, getting distracted by other tasks, feeling incapacitated and unable to move forward – it's often a vicious cycle. When we don't feel motivated, we end up accomplishing very little and this results in us feeling even less motivated than before. And so, the cycle continues.

I prefer to think of motivation in terms of two interrelated levels. The first level is our deeper motivation for completing the PhD, and the second is our day-to-day motivation. Deeper motivation is about re-connecting with your passion and excitement – the thing that first inspired you to pursue your PhD; whereas day-to-day motivation concerns the more immediate challenges of maintaining momentum on a daily basis.

While these two levels of motivation can be viewed as mutually reinforcing, the steps for addressing each are slightly different. Moreover, while both levels are equally important, I would suggest concentrating on underlying motivation first. This is because even if we arm ourselves with the best tips relating to daily motivation, these tips can only be a temporary fix if we've lost our deeper motivation and can no longer identify why we are doing something. If you feel somewhat disconnected from your underlying motivation, try the exercise below:

Exercise: Finding Your 'Why'

Find a quiet space where you can sit comfortably without distractions. Gently take a few deep breaths in and out. When you are ready, start to write down all of the things that are worrying you about your PhD on a few sheets of paper. It could be things like: 'I'm not working fast enough,' 'I'll never get this done,' 'my work isn't good enough,' 'what if I can't find a job when I finish?'. All of the things that are worrying you about the PhD, just write them down.

Now, I'd like you to roll up each scrap of paper into a ball and throw them into a bin, one by one. Imagine yourself feeling lighter and lighter as you throw each scrap away. By going through this process, you are opening up space and quieting that critical voice in your head. If you find that more worried or anxious thoughts are coming to you, continue to repeat this part of the exercise.

Next, when you are ready, I want you to begin to ask

yourself the following questions and be as honest with yourself as possible: Why do I want to do this? What first inspired me to pursue a PhD? Was it a person I met, a place I visited or a book I read? And why did I choose this particular topic? What excited me about this field and this research topic? What can I do with the PhD that I couldn't do without it and what about that really appeals to me? Out of the millions of different things you could have chosen to do, you chose this and that is no accident. Try and reconnect to that initial feeling you had at the outset of the PhD.

Let's now go back to the day your PhD application was accepted. The day you received an offer letter from your university. What time of day was it? How did you feel when you received the good news? Who was the first person that you told? Spend a few moments in this space and really recall your excitement, the sense of joy and anticipation that you felt on that day.

Take a few minutes to reflect on what has come up for you. Was there anything unexpected or surprising in what arose? Many of the students that have gone through this process are able to find their 'why' – that kernel of inspiration or passion that first inspired them to pursue their PhD. The things that tend to get in our way and block us from connecting to that inspiration are our own thoughts, anxieties and worries. But what if you were able to sit in the place of inspiration more regularly? How would it feel to work on your research more often from this place of excitement?

As you go forward, identify whether there are things that remind you of your 'Why'. Something that you can glance at that will automatically enable you to reconnect to why you chose to pursue a PhD. It could be a photo of someone, a book, a painting, an image on your desktop or some other object that reminds you of why you are doing this. If you are able to identify something, perhaps you can keep this item in your work space as a way to tap into your underlying motivation more frequently.

I'm overwhelmed by my work

Even if we are able to regularly reconnect to our deeper-level motivation, completing a PhD can be overwhelming on the best of days. When faced with a seemingly endless amount of work to do and very little time to do it in, the thing that first inspired us to pursue a PhD may not be enough to keep us going. Feeling overwhelmed can make it difficult to know where (or even how) to start.

The roots of overwhelm often lie in an unexpected place and that is our external environment. While it may not always be obvious, our external environment is often a reflection of how we are feeling — such that a chaotic environment may reveal feeling scattered, stressed, and unfocused. In fact, recent research has begun to draw links between a person's physical environment and their sense of wellbeing.

According to a study in the *Personality and Social Psychology Bulletin*, people with cluttered homes and unfinished projects had higher levels of the stress hormone cortisol and were reportedly more fatigued and depressed.[7] The study highlights why it can be difficult to think, let alone live, in a space that is disorganised. Similarly, another investigation has examined the relationship between clutter in the home and our sense of happiness and found that 'clutter had a negative impact on... subjective wellbeing.'[8]

So, if you are looking for a quick remedy to feeling

overwhelmed, it may be worth reflecting on your surroundings. How organised is your work space? Is your desk tidy or filled with clutter? How inviting is your space and how do you tend to feel when you are in it? How often do you tidy and clean your space? Feelings of overwhelm can also be brought on by electronic disarray – for instance, disorganised files on your computer or emails in your inbox. Perhaps some dedicated decluttering time would help make your external environment feel more inviting.

In conjunction with our external environment, it is also important to examine our internal environment – that is, our thoughts in relation to the PhD. It is understandable if the thought of producing 100,000 words feels overwhelming. It is undoubtedly overwhelming. Yet, the truth is that no one producing a thesis actually writes 100,000 words all at once. They write incrementally – one section at a time, one sentence at a time, one word a time. The more we fixate on the final word count, the more overwhelming it starts to feel and, in turn, the harder it becomes to motivate ourselves.

Instead of focusing on the long road ahead, just look to the next step immediately in front of you. In practice, this will involve breaking larger tasks down into smaller, manageable and – most of all – achievable goals. Before you begin a task, write down all the component parts associated with that task and what you consider to be achievable for the day ahead. If something still feels overwhelming, it's usually an indication that the task could be broken down further.

Establishing a system of incentives and rewards can further support your motivation levels and help to alleviate feelings of overwhelm. Start by keeping a list of things that you can reward yourself with as you attain your goals. They don't necessarily need to be big or fancy items – small and inexpensive items are actually ideal for a rewards list. It could be things like: seeing a film, treating yourself to a nice meal, going to a museum or a concert, having your favourite ice cream or a bar of chocolate, or watching something you enjoy on Netflix. These are things you might do anyways, but when you consciously utilise them as a way to reward yourself, they tend to take on a new meaning.

By rewarding yourself regularly in this way, you not only give yourself additional motivation to complete a task, you also practice better self-care. Whereas many students slip into the paradigm of beating themselves up in relation to their work, rewarding yourself regularly will remind you to be gentle with yourself. This can make the entire PhD experience a lot more enjoyable. The headway you make towards achieving your goal – however big or small the step may seem – represents progress. Not only are these steps important to acknowledge, they are worth celebrating in their own right.

What's the best way to structure my time?

PhD students have a considerable degree of freedom when it comes to determining their schedules. In contrast to a conventional 9-to-5 job, most doctoral students aren't required to be on campus, nor are they expected to work for a specific number of hours each day. And no one is looking over their shoulder to monitor when they work and for how long. While this freedom could be viewed as a blessing, for many it is also somewhat of a curse. Without set hours many students end up working even more than they would in a regular job. Not only do they rarely give themselves breaks or proper time off, when they do they are often racked with work guilt.

Working all day – and sometimes all night – makes it challenging to sustain our motivation. It doesn't necessarily equate with greater levels of productivity either. In fact, it can often mean the opposite. Most of us have certain peak hours where we tend to be most productive, as well as lull hours where it can be challenging to get anything done. For instance, I know that I am at my most productive in the early hours of the morning and that I experience a lull around mid-afternoon. With that in mind, I've stopped trying to force myself to work at all hours of the day. I now accept the fact that there are natural peaks and lulls throughout my day, and try to work with that reality instead of fighting against it. I carve out early mornings for work that involves a lot of focus and then save administrative tasks and chores for the afternoon, which are by nature less demanding but equally important to do.

When it comes to structuring your time, it can be helpful to be aware of what your peak and lull hours are, and to schedule tasks accordingly. Take a moment and reflect on what your working patterns are and see if you can make any shifts to your schedule to better utilise your hours of peak productivity.

In addition to making the most of my peak and lull hours, I've also noticed that I am most motivated when I consciously approach my working day as a cycle, segmented into three mutually reinforcing phases. The three phases are **before** I begin working, **during** my working hours, and **after** I've finished working for the day.

The **Before Phase** involves setting myself up for the day ahead. This requires addressing practical matters like organizing my work space, while also paying attention to my mind-set, exploring any resistance to work that comes up, identifying incentives and rewards, and reconnecting to what inspires me.

The **During Phase** is about enhancing my concentration and focus in order to make the most of my working hours. This will involve setting realistic and achievable targets, overcoming perfectionist tendencies, and adopting strategies to make me more present with my work (such as the Pomodoro Technique).

The **After Phase** consists of detaching from my work. Stepping into this space can be a challenge for many and it is admittedly the phase that comes the least naturally to me. In fact, the notion of detaching simply didn't exist for me when I was completing my doctorate. What I've come to realize is that detaching is not a luxury, but an essential component of my working day. Not only is it crucial for my wellbeing, it also gives my mind a break and allows me to return to my work feeling reinvigorated and refreshed.

It is not important how much time is spent in each phase. In reality, the amount of time devoted to each will likely vary day-to-day. Some days I spend less time in the Before Phase and am able to jump straight into my work. Other days, I may need more time in the After Phase, particularly if I've been working on something challenging. What matters most is consciously and deliberately moving through each phase of the cycle and observing its main components: getting set up for the working day, making the most of my working hours, and having an opportunity to properly detach from work at the end of the day. For additional tips on each phase of the Daily Work Cycle, see the *Doctoral De-Stress* Book Bonuses page on academease.org.

I'm reluctant to take time off

No matter how much we may love our work, we need to be able to step away from it from time-to-time. When I was a student I was extremely reluctant to take breaks and vacations for fear that I would fall behind in my work. I remember feeling like I had so much to do and was constantly wishing I had more time available to work. How could I possibly imagine taking time off? Eventually, I started to do what many students end up doing and that is bringing my work with me on my holidays.

What I learned was that mixing my vacation time with the expectation to work is a recipe for disaster. Not only did I not complete any of the work that I had hoped to do, I also didn't fully relax or enjoy myself when I was on holiday either. It was tough to relax when I knew I had a suitcase filled with books waiting to be read. This meant that there was no actual benefit to going on holiday and afterwards I would return feeling even more stressed out than before I had left. So rather ironically, it was after I came back from my holidays that I felt most in need of taking a break.

For PhD students, the resistance to taking time off most likely stems from the belief that we don't deserve to take a break, or more specifically, that we haven't done enough to earn that break. In this sense, it is our own self-judgment that precludes us from taking time off. Although it may seem counterintuitive, it is precisely in those instances where we feel least deserving of a break that we would probably benefit most from taking one. Even if we view time off as an unwanted distraction from our pressing PhD work, in actuality, proper time off is something that sustains and supports our capacity to work. Distance makes the heart grow fonder and that applies to our work as well!

While I've come around to the idea that taking time off benefits me and my capacity to work, it doesn't necessarily make it any easier to wholeheartedly embrace that time. We so often hear about the virtues of 'switching off' from work as though it were simply a question of flicking a switch. This is, however, another aspect of PhD life that is distinct from having a conventional job. Most PhD students live and breathe their research and have it on their minds whether they are actively working on it or not. The level of focus and mental energy we expend on our academic work can make it challenging to transition into relaxion mode. Here are a few simple steps to help you transition into downtime with greater ease:

Step 1: Set an end to your work day in advance

The first step is to set an end to your work day before you even start working. Most of us are taught the virtues of being a hard worker from a very young age, so the notion of consciously and deliberately taking time off work – rather than taking time off when we reach burnout or exhaustion – can feel quite alien. Yet the value of carving out some non-working time in your day and making this non-negotiable will far outweigh any initial reluctance and discomfort with this step. Not only will this give you something to look forward to, having an end time set in advance will help you to make the most of your working hours, which in itself will ease some of the resistance to taking time off.

Step 2: Find an activity unrelated to your work

Now that you've set an end to your work day, it's important to fill that space with something other than work. If we don't fill that time, it is more likely that work will creep back into the space we've carved out. Try and select an activity that is completely unrelated to your work. It might be a long-lost hobby, a sport, a craft, a language or anything else that you've been interested in trying but haven't managed to find the time for. At this point I hear a lot of people saying 'I can't afford to do a hobby or take time off each day... I have so much work to do', which is something I'll address in the next step.

Step 3: Give yourself permission

Much of the resistance to switching off stems from the fact that many of us don't feel like we can afford the time off or that we even deserve it. With so much to do, the prospect of deliberately switching off can quickly develop into feelings of guilt. The next step I recommend is to override the feelings of guilt by actively giving yourself permission to take time off. If this step feels like a struggle, an affirmation can be useful. It could be something along the lines of the following: 'I'm proud of what I've done today'; 'I deserve to take some time off'; 'My work will still be here in the morning.'

Step 4: Adopt a transition activity

Sometimes the challenge with switching off relates directly to the type of work we are engaged in. The nature of PhD research makes it difficult to go directly from the lab, the library or the office into relaxing. In order to give our brains some space to recalibrate, it can be helpful to try and adopt a transition activity between our work and our downtime. Exercising or even a brisk walk can be a great way to transition between work and downtime. Another good transition activity is grocery shopping, as it gives our brain another task to focus on as we start to wind down.

Step 5: Carry a notebook with you

Even if we were to strictly observe the above steps, our thoughts may still gravitate towards work. This isn't necessarily a bad thing – some of the best ideas I had during my PhD came to me when I wasn't actively trying to work on it. This is why I often recommend that students carry a notebook with them. That way, if an idea comes to you, you can quickly make a note of it and return to it the following day instead of getting caught up in that thought when you are trying to relax. This allows you to remain receptive to thoughts and ideas without having them derail your downtime.

I feel like I'm not making progress

The relationship between progress and motivation can either operate as a virtuous cycle or a vicious one. For example, when we feel as though we are making progress, we experience an automatic boost to our motivation. In contrast, when we judge that we haven't made sufficient progress it becomes exceptionally difficult to sustain any forward movement. In effect, we become stuck.

The difficulty with progress at the PhD level is that the assessment of whether or not we've made any is almost entirely a subjective one. Aside from those relatively infrequent assessments during the course of a PhD, including upgrade panels or transfer vivas, there is very little evaluation of our work. Even the interaction we have with our supervisors and their assessments of our work is limited and irregular at best. The majority of the time, we are left to our own devices, which means that it is up to us to assess our progress on a day-to-day basis.

In the absence of any other obvious yardstick to assess progress, I've noticed that the default setting for PhD students is to rely on their overall word count as a supposedly objective measure. If the aim is to write a thesis of 100,000 words, surely the number of words we have produced by the end of the day can be a proxy for whether or not we are on track?

Although your word count may seem like the most obvious and reliable way to measure your progress, there is so much more that goes into producing a thesis than simply writing a set number of words. There are days when you might not write very much, or anything at all, but that doesn't mean you aren't making progress. Consider going to the library and skimming 10 articles and realising only two are relevant to your thesis. This could be a day where you feel like you haven't progressed at all, but sorting through literature and deciding what will be included in your final bibliography is indeed forward momentum. The trouble with counting words is that it is solely outcome focused, and goes back to the outcome-oriented approach discussed in Chapter 1.

Even if we dispense with word count as an indicator of progress, we still need an alternative yardstick to determine that we are on track, or at the very least, a supplementary one. One option would be to utilise the PhD Process Journal discussed earlier in conjunction with, or instead of, relying on word count. The journal could, for instance, include all of the actions short of writing that still bring us closer to completing our thesis. Writing it out may help us to feel forward movement on tasks that may otherwise go unnoticed. It may also give a more realistic picture of our progress than one based on word count alone. The example of going to the library and determining sources to incorporate in our bibliography could be included as an entry.

A further option for assessing progress could be entirely time-focused. For instance, you might wish to make a note of how many Pomodoro rounds you manage to complete on a given day (discussed in Chapter 2). Since a Pomodoro round would count as uninterrupted time that you are putting into your thesis, it is a helpful way to keep track of your productivity. It also enables you to put much less emphasis on the task – which in the case of a thesis may seem never-ending – and focus more on the hours that are put into it. A variation of this could be something like the Forest App, which allows you to physically see the progress you are making on the basis of the time invested.[9]

A final way to keep track of your progress without exclusively relying on your word count is to work with an accountability partner. By communicating on a regular basis, you and your accountability partner can mutually support each other in achieving your goals. The idea would be that you have a set meeting to determine your goals and a further check in to evaluate your progress. It might also be an opportunity to discuss any challenges that came up for you and to brainstorm possible solutions to those challenges. Depending on what your needs are, you can check in with your accountability partner daily, weekly or even monthly.

As the above approaches highlight, even when you feel like you aren't making progress on your PhD, chances are you probably are. While word count provides one possible yardstick for measuring progress, the alternative approaches explored in this section tend to provide a better reflection of PhD progress. What they allow for is a much more comprehensive account of the work that actually goes into producing a PhD.

Chapter Three Takeaways

☐ Motivation is best thought of on two interrelated levels. The first level is our deeper motivation for completing the PhD, and the second is our day-to-day motivation. Deeper motivation is about re-connecting with your passion and excitement – the thing that first inspired you to pursue your PhD; whereas day-to-day motivation concerns the more immediate challenges of maintaining momentum on a daily basis. If you feel somewhat disconnected from your deeper motivation, try the exercise in this chapter 'Finding Your Why'.

☐ Establishing a system of incentives and rewards can further support your motivation levels and help to alleviate feelings of overwhelm. Start by keeping a list of things that you can reward yourself with as you attain your goals.

☐ It can be helpful to approach your working day as a cycle, segmented into three mutually reinforcing phases. What matters most is consciously and deliberately moving through each phase of the cycle and observing its main components: getting set up for the working day, making the most of my working hours, and having an opportunity to properly detach from work at the end of the day. For specific tips on each phase of the Daily Work Cycle, see the *Doctoral De-Stress* Book Bonuses page on academease.org.

☐ Most PhD students live and breathe their research and have it on their minds whether they are actively working on it or not. The level of focus and mental energy we expend on our academic work can make it challenging to switch off. To help ease into your downtime try the following tips: set an end to your work day in advance; find an activity unrelated to your work; give yourself permission to take time off; adopt a transition activity; and, carry a notebook with you for any ideas that come up during your leisure time.

☐ While your word count provides one possible yardstick for measuring progress, the alternative approaches explored in this chapter (such as journaling, a time-focused approach or an accountability partner) tend to offer a more accurate account of PhD progress.

4

SUPERVISOR STRESS

I don't feel supported by my supervisor

The relationship we have with our academic supervisors can make or break the PhD experience. Whenever I ask a group of students to identify their number one challenge throughout the PhD, supervisor relationships come out on top. There does seem to be something in the nature of the supervisor-supervisee relationship that feels especially prone to discord.

Unfortunately, despite the centrality of this relationship to the PhD experience, there is no instruction manual detailing how we should interact with our supervisors, what can be expected from this relationship, or how to handle any prospective disputes that might arise. It is often down to the individuals involved to determine how this important relationship will operate. This leads to considerable variation in individual experiences.

Sometimes the relationship works very well and a student is fortunate to end up with a supervisor that is encouraging, attentive and easy to communicate with. At the opposite end of the spectrum are the horror stories involving supervisors that may be anything ranging from unresponsive and absent to overly controlling or even aggressive.

While it may seem as though attaining a positive supervisor-supervisee relationship is simply a roll of the dice, not everything should be left to chance. There is always scope to improve this relationship irrespective of what stage you are at in the PhD. The key to improving your relationship with your supervisor is to begin with an honest inventory of where things are at.

Step one is to reflect on what is working well. What things do you admire or respect about your supervisor? In what ways is your relationship with your supervisor functioning well? Step two is to consider aspects of the relationship that you'd like to shift. Where are you not receiving the support you require from your supervisor? What would you like to see improve? It could, for instance, be more frequent contact, clearer feedback or joint meetings with your secondary supervisor. Whatever it might be, try and identify specific things that you would like to see shift.

Next comes the part that may be uncomfortable for many students and that is to ask your supervisor for the support that you need. It may seem like an obvious point, but many students don't feel like they are in a position to ask their supervisors for support. There may be a reluctance to speak up given that your supervisor is more senior. The last thing we want is to create a conflict, further aggravate the relationship, or do anything to tarnish our reputations. It can feel as though there is just too much at stake to speak up and so the default position becomes to accept the situation as it is, irrespective of whether it's working or not. On closer inspection, however, there are actually plenty more reasons to speak up and ask for support than not.

First, the perception that you may have of the situation with your supervisor may not be evident to them at all. They may see things in a different way or simply have no idea that they have been neglecting to fully support you. The fact is that our supervisors cannot read our minds, so it is up to us to communicate our needs to them. Each of us is responsible for ourselves, so if we aren't getting the support we need and yet continue to stay quiet, we are equally liable for the shortfalls in the relationship as they are.

Second, although the resistance to speaking up may stem from a fear that it may lead to a conflict, there is no reason to expect that it will. After all, what you are asking for is reasonable. If you frame your request clearly and directly, in a calm manner, and without being accusatory or confrontational, it is simply you speaking up about what your needs are. There is nothing inherently aggressive or conflictual about that.

Finally, while the desire to avoid conflict may seem like a powerful rationale for accepting the status-quo, there is an immense cost to staying quiet, and that is the internal conflict that this will generate within you. To carry on and slog away with your work in the absence of feeling fully supported will undoubtedly taint your experience of the PhD. After all, pursuing a doctorate is not an easy undertaking. It requires dedication and diligence, not to mention a considerable investment of time and money. You owe it to yourself to do everything you can to ensure that you are fully supported throughout this process.

I disagree with some of my supervisor's advice

What happens if your supervisor advises you to take your thesis in a direction that you don't agree with? Whether it's integrating new literature, changing your methodology, or selecting different case studies, your supervisor may have particularly strong opinions about aspects of your thesis. If you end up following their advice – whether you agree with their ideas or not – your thesis is likely to end up looking quite different to what you had envisaged.

The fact that you might feel forced to change an aspect of your thesis reveals something significant about the supervisor-supervisee relationship. Without being aware of it, most students operate with their supervisors on the basis of an employer-employee dynamic. When your employer asks you to do a piece of work for them, most employees typically go ahead and do that work without questioning the logic of it or whether it makes sense to them. It's an instruction to be acted upon, a directive, rather than something that is open to conversation and debate. When this dynamic is transposed onto a PhD setting, our supervisors become the employers and students in turn become the dutiful employees. As such, when a supervisor advises a student to go in a particular direction with their research, most students interpret this advice as a directive, with minimal scope for further dialogue.

The problem with operating on this basis is that your supervisor is not your employer and it's important to ask yourself whether you've been inadvertently behaving as though they are. If you have been, don't beat yourself up

– it's a common dynamic I see with many students and it's not too late to try and reverse it. It begins with you starting to own your PhD project. Supervisors are there to guide you through the process, but at the end of the day, it's down to you to take ownership of your project and shape it the way that you want.

Hold firm to the vision you have for your PhD project. If you don't like the direction that is suggested by your supervisor, don't hesitate to discuss it with them. Ask for clarification as to why they would like you to shift a particular aspect of the thesis and make sure you are fully on board with it before you agree to any substantive changes. Deferring to their vision for your project is likely to make you much less enthusiastic about your PhD as a whole, and perhaps even come to resent it.

The same applies to differences of opinion you may have with your supervisor about non-thesis related matters. Things like whether you should get teaching experience during your PhD, attend conferences, pursue publishing opportunities, and which jobs to apply for. Countless students perceive opinions on such issues as directives from their supervisors, when in actuality they probably have a lot more control over their choices than they believe.

While your supervisor may have opinions about each of these issues, it's important to remember that it is just an opinion. The world may have changed a lot since your supervisor did their PhD and, therefore, the advice they are able to offer you may be somewhat limited. Graciously accept their advice when it is offered, but try not to treat everything they say as gospel. Talk to others and, above all, follow your own instincts. Ultimately, it is up to you to determine these matters for yourself.

If you do feel like you need their support on a particular matter, it's best to approach any discussions on the front foot, rather than feeling like you require their permission or wholesale approval. Be mindful of how you frame your conversations with them and try to avoid slipping back into employer-employee mode. You may not end up in agreement with your supervisor on everything and that's OK. A good working relationship is not based on avoiding differences of opinion altogether, but in being able to mutually respect those differences when they do occur.

My supervisor's comments are harsh

In an ideal scenario our supervisors would be tremendously supportive and enthusiastic about our research. Every meeting with them would leave us feeling boosted. Unfortunately, the reality often falls short of this ideal. Rather than experiencing elevated interactions with our supervisors, the feedback we receive from them may appear harsh and leave us feeling distraught about our work. In such cases, we may be left wondering what the point is and whether or not it's even worth pursuing our research.

While no one likes to have their work criticised, hearing negative feedback about our PhD research can feel especially bad. Given the personal nature of the topics we research, many students tend to overidentify with their work. As such, any negative feedback regarding our projects can lead us to internalise these comments and make it mean something about ourselves. A further reason why we might not take negative feedback particularly well is that most of us are simply not used to hearing it. If you are enrolled in a PhD programme chances are that you have excelled academically. You've grown accustomed to being complimented on your work, instead of having someone point out all of its shortcomings.

If you find yourself on the receiving end of negative comments about your work, it can be helpful to remind yourself that this comes with the territory of doing a PhD. As uncomfortable and awful as it may feel, it is your supervisor's job to spot potential holes in your research and if they weren't doing this, they wouldn't be a very good supervisor. Try your best not to personalize their comments. Remember that it's much better to receive negative comments on drafts of your thesis than during your viva.

It is, of course, still unpleasant to hear negative feedback about your work and you wouldn't be alone if the prospect of harsh feedback filled you with dread. What I recommend is to begin by giving yourself a bit of time and space away from any feedback you receive. At the very least, give it 24 hours. Not only does feedback always feel worse at first sight, you will likely perceive it less harshly when you read it with fresh eyes.

Next, whenever you feel ready, sit down and calmly sift through all of the feedback. Go through each comment one by one. Try and filter out how it is delivered and ask yourself two key questions. First: 'Is this particular comment clear?' In other words, does it make sense to you? If, for instance, the comments are confusing, don't hesitate to ask your supervisor for clarity. If the feedback is clear, the second question to ask yourself is: 'Will this feedback ultimately strengthen my project?' If the answer is yes, it may help you get less wrapped up in the specifics of the comment and come to view it more constructively.

If you are still feeling unhappy with your supervisor's

feedback, and if it's becoming a pattern every time you share drafts of your work, you may need to do something about this. It may not be possible to fundamentally change how your supervisor delivers feedback. However, if their comments are leaving you distraught, it would be worth asking them to highlight what they do like about your draft chapters, or indeed your thesis as a whole. This is a subtle way to ask for a bit more balance in their assessments of your work.

While it may feel awkward to you, as though you are fishing for a compliment from them, there should be no shame at all in requesting balanced feedback. Your supervisor may mean no harm and could be completely unaware of how their comments appear, or the broader impact their feedback is having on you. Not only will asking for balanced feedback better enable you to put their comments in context, it may also serve as a gentle reminder to your supervisor to be more encouraging in general.

My supervisor is too easy on me

While no student wants to hear exclusively negative comments about their work, it can be equally unhelpful to have a supervisor that solely praises their work. At first glance, the prospect of regularly receiving positive feedback may not seem like a problem at all. After all, who wouldn't want to have their work praised? As much as we might like the sound of a supervisor that is consistently positive about our work, it may start to feel like our supervisor is being too easy on us. In an ideal situation, your supervisor would strike a balance between providing criticism, which is constructive in nature, and offering praise when it is warranted.

Among the many reasons that we pursue research at the doctoral level is to become authorities on our respective topics. Being repeatedly told that our work is great doesn't exactly challenge us to improve our work, sharpen our skills, or further hone our knowledge of the field. Feeling challenged is a crucial part of pursuing a PhD, and one that our supervisors should have a key role in facilitating.

Moreover, students also look to their supervisors to act as a barometer for their progress. They do so because, during a PhD, there are few ways for a student to determine whether they are on the right track. Aside from yearly upgrade panels, there are virtually no avenues of assessment available at the PhD level until the viva. This highlights the importance of a supervisor that provides thoroughly honest assessments of their student's work. If, for instance, a supervisor has only complimentary things to say, how can we really be sure we are on the right track?

So where does all of this leave those who feel their supervisors are being too easy on them? If you have a sense that you aren't being sufficiently challenged, it may require you to have a conversation with your supervisor in which you explicitly ask them to highlight any limitations they see in your work, or areas for improvement. Your willingness to hear constructive criticism of your work may encourage your supervisor to start offering more substantive feedback in subsequent conversations.

In addition to requesting some more constructive feedback from your supervisor, I would also explore alternative avenues for sharing your work. This might involve exchanging drafts of your work with peers, reaching out to academics at other universities, or interacting with colleagues at conferences. Exposing your project to other people and perspectives will strengthen your work while making you less reliant on the feedback of one person.

Far too many students come to rely exclusively on their supervisors for support, inspiration, and advice throughout their PhDs. While there is no denying that the supervisor-supervisee relationship is a vital component of successfully completing your PhD, putting all of your focus on a single person not only puts a lot of pressure on that relationship, it can sometimes set you up for disappointment. Do what you can to cultivate the best possible relationship with your supervisor, but don't hesitate to simultaneously cultivate connections beyond the supervisor-supervisee bubble.

The relationship with my supervisor is no longer working

It may be that you've tried everything in your power to improve the relationship with your supervisor, but have regrettably concluded that the current situation is no longer sustainable. If you've reached this point, it may be time to explore the possibility of making alternative supervision arrangements.

Having to switch supervisors in the midst of pursuing a doctorate is not an easy undertaking. Given the centrality of the supervisor-supervisee relationship to the PhD process, experiencing a rupture of this kind can be deeply unsettling and emotionally exhausting. If you find yourself in this situation, it's important to be gentle with yourself as you go through this. Although changing supervisors is not ideal, it does happen. Remember that you aren't the first student to be in this predicament and you certainly won't be the last.

Since the decision to switch supervisors is not likely to be reversible, it is important to explore all of your options before initiating a change. It may, for instance, be worth considering whether there is anything you can salvage out of your current arrangement. This may involve taking a more functional approach towards supervision, in which your interactions with your supervisor are limited to those that are essential. On the basis of this more functional arrangement, you would accept that the relationship has its limits, let go of any expectations and know that your association with this person is temporary. Your sole purpose in communicating with your supervisor is to get you through to the PhD finish line.

A further option would be to supplement your existing supervision arrangement by bringing on board a secondary supervisor (if you don't already have one). You could select someone you feel comfortable around who is genuinely supportive of your project. An additional supervisor may prove to be a useful counterweight to your existing supervisor.

If switching supervisors requires you to go through an endless bureaucratic procedure, or if you are concerned about causing offence to your current supervisor, you could potentially make the switch on a more informal basis. This would allow you to maintain your current supervisor on paper, while informally acquiring the support of another supervisor in practice.

As is evident, when it comes to structuring the working arrangements between you and your PhD supervisor, there are plenty of possibilities. There are a variety of different ways we can work with our PhD supervisors and no one-size-fits-all approach. Therefore, if the current situation really isn't working well, it is within your power to initiate a change.

Even if the worst has happened and you've fallen out with your PhD supervisor, that person may still be one of your greatest teachers – not in a traditional sense, but in terms of the life-lessons you have learned through interacting with them.

By not making things easy, your supervisor has helped you to develop certain qualities within yourself that may have otherwise remained dormant. Things like self-confidence, the courage to stand up for yourself, and a willingness to set boundaries. These are the types of qualities that can only be cultivated through difficult interactions. Therefore, as much as we might prefer to have had an easier time with our supervisors, the fact that they have been challenging actually offers us an invaluable opportunity to grow.

For a downloadable summary of my top tips for enhancing the relationship with your academic supervisor, see the *Doctoral De-Stress* Book Bonuses page on academease.org.

Chapter Four Takeaways

☐ Many students approach their interactions with academic supervisors through the lens of an employer/employee relationship. This is a wholly misguided approach in the context of a PhD. A supervisor is simply not equivalent to a boss or a line manager.

☐ You may not end up in agreement with your supervisor on everything and that's OK. A good working relationship is not based on avoiding differences of opinion altogether, but in being able to mutually respect those differences when they do occur.

☐ It may not be possible to fundamentally change how your supervisor delivers feedback. However, if their comments are leaving you distraught it would be worth asking them for a bit more balance in their assessments of your work.

☐ Far too many students come to rely exclusively on their supervisors for support, inspiration and advice throughout their PhDs. Putting all of your focus on a single person not only puts a lot of pressure on that relationship, it can sometimes set you up for disappointment. Do what you can to cultivate the best possible relationship with your supervisor, but don't hesitate to simultaneously cultivate connections beyond your supervisor-supervisee bubble.

☐ There are a variety of different ways we can work with our PhD supervisors and no one-size-fits-all approach. If we aren't getting the support we need, and yet continue to stay quiet, we are equally liable for the shortfalls in the relationship as they are.

5

ROADBLOCKS AND DETOURS
ON THE PHD PATH

Unforeseen circumstances are hindering my PhD progress

When we first embark on the journey towards obtaining a PhD, we do so with the best intentions. We envisage a smooth path ahead of us and the key milestones we intend to reach along the way. What we don't anticipate are the unexpected situations that throw us off course – things that obstruct our path or force us to make a detour.

On average it takes approximately four years to complete a PhD and there is certainly a lot that can happen within that time. We are often different people by the time we come out on the other side. Our personal circumstances may change, our families may endure a crisis, or we could end up experiencing financial hardship. The roadblocks we encounter could also be directly related to our research. Perhaps the topic we had decided to write on is no longer feasible or we've run into problems with our supervisor.

Although we can take steps to mitigate certain roadblocks, others are impossible to foresee. The COVID-19 Pandemic is an excellent example of this. No one saw it coming, yet it had a momentous impact on all higher education institutions. Regular working patterns were disturbed by the requirement to work from home, research funding suddenly came under threat with the economic downturn, field work was disrupted by travel restrictions, and universities were forced to shift to a virtual learning environment overnight. No amount of planning or foresight could have prepared us for this crisis. Every student pursuing their PhD could feel the impact of this situation and had to find ways to adapt.

Whatever type of roadblock we encounter, from a personal crisis to a global pandemic, the consequences from a PhD perspective are almost always the same. Most roadblocks on the PhD path result in delays, which will likely mean requesting an extension or an interruption of studies. In other words, an already lengthy process gets drawn out further.

The prospect of a protracted PhD, irrespective of the reasons that necessitate it, can be a difficult pill for a doctoral student to swallow. In fact, I've never come across a PhD student that is content with the amount of time their PhD journey has taken them. Most tend to despair at the length of time that it takes and judge themselves rather harshly for not being able to complete it more swiftly. As such, the notion of requesting additional time is not likely to be greeted with enthusiasm.

Some of the concern with prolonging the PhD derives from a fear that our work may become outdated if we submit it later than planned. Nevertheless, the time frame is less important than it may at first appear. For instance, if you select any piece of work, there will always be scope for updating, improving, or revising it in line with recent developments. Academic research is, by its very nature, dynamic and continuously evolving – never really 'done'. It is simply a snapshot at a specific moment in time and, therefore, the time frame for completing your thesis is likely to be much more flexible than you have come to believe.

A further reason why a delay may not seem appealing stems from the stigma of finishing behind your peers. If you end up taking more time and your peers finish before you, what will it look like? And, more crucially, what will it mean? Although you began your PhD journey with a peer group, it is important to remember that you are each on individual paths. Every project is unique, as is each student's working patterns and personal circum-stances. Any supposed competition between you and your peers is more imagined than real. The bottom line is that whether you submit before or after them makes absolutely no difference at all. The PhD is not a race to the finish line.

Taking more time to finish your thesis as a result of a roadblock is by no means something to be embarrassed about. When you look back at your completed PhD, the fact that you persisted despite challenges is a testament to your dedication and perseverance. Staying the course in the face of roadblocks is something to be proud of and celebrated.

I've had to significantly change my project

Sometimes the types of roadblock we experience during a PhD precipitate not only a delay but also a fundamental change in the direction of our research. This can be equally frustrating for a student to come to terms with.

The vast majority of students begin their PhDs with a very clear idea of what they want to do. In fact, most PhD programmes require applicants to submit a research proposal as part of their application, and it is on this basis that a student is offered a place.

Given the vital role of a research proposal in terms of gaining admission into a doctoral programme, it is understandable why students attach great importance to it. The proposal serves as both a road map for students and a guide for executing their research. In reality, however, most doctoral students do not stick to their research proposals. The end result of their PhD can often look quite different when contrasted to what was stated in their original plan. How do we account for the discrepancy between a student's research proposal and their completed doctorate?

The initial plan we come into a PhD programme with is often an idealized version of what we imagine our research journey to be, before we have taken any steps on the path. As soon as we begin to get further into our research, not only do we get a sense of where the project needs to go, we also start to realize how much we don't know about our topics. Gaps in our initial proposal become evident, new questions emerge, and different avenues of inquiry start to open up. None of these things would have been apparent before starting the PhD and it is really only by getting further into your topic that such things come into view.

In this sense, any departure from your original proposal is a natural part of pursuing a PhD. You may decide of your own accord that your proposal was overly ambitious and requires paring down; that there is a substantial piece missing in your research design; or that an emerging trend needs to be incorporated into your project.

While changing the direction of your PhD project may be your decision, it is still bound to feel a little uncomfortable. This is particularly the case if changing direction will involve discarding any material you have already produced, as it so often does. It can be extremely frustrating to dispense with material that may admittedly no longer fit, but which you nonetheless spent a considerable amount of time on. Unfortunately, no one warns you prior to starting a PhD just how much material you won't end up using in the final version. It can easily feel as though you've wasted your time and created more work for yourself, but it's important to continue to focus on the bigger picture.

Even with the frustration of discarding material, any changes to the initial idea for your research should still be viewed in a generally positive light. Aside from being a natural part of the PhD journey, changing direction is actually a sign of progress. When you get to the point of determining the most appropriate direction for your research – and are confident enough to change the project accordingly – what it really means is that your expertise and knowledge base are developing. Try not to despair if you've had to significantly alter your project. You are much closer to the finish line than you think.

Someone got there first and is researching my topic

If I were to take a survey of doctoral students and ask them to list their top fears, discovering that another person is researching their topic would undoubtedly be on that list. A PhD is meant to be an original piece of research, contributing to the advancement of knowledge in a specific field. The prospect of anyone treading into your specialised research area can understandably feel quite threatening. And while there is never a good time to discover that someone has published on your topic, a nightmare scenario would be to stumble across the others person's research when you are nearing completion.

The fear of someone else treading into the boundaries of our research can encourage students to become territorial – even possessive – about their work. It can also breed a reluctance to share ideas with others and make a student wary of presenting their work in public. As such, they end up missing out on crucial opportunities to share their ideas and receive feedback.

A doctorate takes several years to complete and the fact of the matter is that you aren't going to be able to control what is or isn't published within that time frame. Trying to control what effectively can't be controlled is exhausting. Moreover, carrying around the fear of someone else getting there first throughout the duration of your PhD is an additional stress during an already stressful time.

While it is understandable that you'd want your project to be unique, the fact that others may be publishing on the same topic may not be as problematic as you think. For instance, someone writing on your topic demonstrates that you are onto something. You are working on a topic that clearly resonates with others.

PhDs are often very specialised and at times it can feel like quite a lonesome endeavour. There will be few people who really understand what you are working on or its broader significance. Discovering that someone else is working on your topic may, therefore, provide you with a prospective colleague to converse with.

It is also highly likely that, despite any similarities, the way they've explored the topic is different to your approach. This is because you have your own unique way of approaching your topic, which cannot be replicated. Even if their topic is exactly the same as yours, the way they have executed it will be different. Engaging with someone else's interpretation of your topic may allow you to further solidify what is unique about your approach. In this respect, another perspective on your topic could actually strengthen your project.

Finally, the fact that someone else is examining a closely related – or even identical – topic as your project is not sufficient grounds to undermine your claim of originality. The condition of originality is often misinterpreted in overly stringent terms, but it is important to put the requirement in its proper context. When it comes to PhD theses, very few projects are completely groundbreaking.

For all of these reasons, discovering that someone else has published on your thesis topic may not be as disastrous as it first appears. As with everything, your own perspective counts for a lot, so try and see it as an opportunity rather than a roadblock.

I keep getting in my own way

Many people experience a certain degree of negative thinking in relation to themselves and their work. The trouble is that when a specific thought pattern is practiced over and over again, it starts to form a core belief system. This is the power of our thoughts. In this respect, the biggest barrier to our progress is not something that comes from outside of us; it is actually our own thinking that allows us to get in our own way. In order to break free of negative thought patterns, we first need to understand more about the nature of thought.

It has been estimated that we have over 60,000 thoughts a day. At times our thoughts seem to emerge out of nowhere and we appear to have little control over our thinking. However, by becoming more aware of our thought patterns, we can consciously begin to choose thoughts that feel better.

Imagine a thought as a rock at the top of a mountain. As the rock begins to roll down from the top of that mountain it gathers more and more momentum, and it accelerates. This is exactly what happens with our thoughts when we are feeling off.

We may have one thought that doesn't feel good and, before we know it, the pace of that thought tends to gather momentum and leaves us feeling worse off. We may start off by thinking: 'I'm having difficulty writing this chapter', and that leads into: 'It's not going to be good enough anyways'; 'My whole thesis probably won't be good enough'; 'I'll never get a job when I finish my PhD – if I ever finish'; 'What's the point?' etc.

Notice how specific these thoughts are. Very often this type of thought pattern occurs so quickly without us even noticing. The key to overcoming a spiral of negative thought momentum is to first become aware of it. Our emotions are often the best indicator of this – when we aren't feeling good, it's usually an indication that we are experiencing negative thought momentum.

Once we become aware, we can consciously try and break negative thought momentum. The best way to do this is to grab a pen and paper and actively write down slower and more positive thoughts.

For example, from the initial worry of, 'I'm having difficulty writing this chapter', we could remind ourselves of the following: 'I have produced quality work in the past'; 'I enjoy my research'; 'Things have a way of working out.' Whereas negative thought momentum tends to be quite specific and zoomed-in, these statements take a more zoomed-out perspective of the situation. They typically offer a more accurate account of the situation, and as a consequence, they tend to feel a lot better. We all have unlimited access to these better-feeling thoughts. It's often just a matter of which thoughts we choose to focus on in any given moment.

When we are really caught up in a spiral of negative thought momentum, the prospect of slowing down our thoughts and getting more general may feel too challenging. When this occurs, there are plenty of other things we can try to break negative thought momentum, all of which involve getting off the topic that is causing you to spiral by doing something completely different. It could be anything you enjoy doing (cooking, reading, exercising, listening to music, napping, meditating, seeing a film, connecting with a friend) or even a chore that will help distract you for a short time. Whatever the task is, you'll be in a much better position to access slower, more general thoughts after taking some time out for yourself.

I feel like quitting my PhD

Pursuing a PhD is a huge investment of time and energy. The years of hard work that you put into it involve a lot of sacrifice. People around you may not entirely understand the ups and downs of the process, or why you might not be as available, which can make it quite an isolating experience. And as thrilling as it is to make progress on your PhD, it can also be slow moving progress. For all these reasons, it's perfectly understandable to question your commitment to the PhD. Even those with no real intention of calling it quits may still entertain the thought of walking away from time to time.

If, however, the feeling is coming up consistently for you, then it's worth paying attention to. At the very least, take it as an opportunity to check in with yourself and ensure you are still doing your PhD for the right reasons. Sometimes we continue on the path we are on for all the wrong reasons. It may be out of fear, habit or even guilt of disappointing others if we quit. It may also be down to uncertainty over what else we would do instead. However, it's not enough to continue with your PhD simply because you started it. If it is no longer making you happy, it's worth considering what would need to change for you to feel better about it.

If the problem turns out to be more fundamental, like you aren't enjoying your research and really want to do something else with your life, it's important to recognise that before investing more time and energy into your studies. Re-evaluating your commitment to the PhD may also be part of a larger re-evaluation of your life, where you consider what matters to you and how obtaining your PhD either does or doesn't fit into that. In any case, before making a final decision, it may be worth giving yourself some time off to better access how you are feeling, or even going part-time while you weigh your options. This can give you the necessary distance to determine what you really want.

If you choose to seek out others' advice before making your decision, remember that people tend to be heavily biased by their own experiences. Like most major decisions, you probably already know deep down what is best for you. It's really just a matter of being honest with yourself by first acknowledging and then owning how you are feeling.

Sometimes we persist with things that aren't working because we are concerned about how it will look or what others will think of us. But if pursuing a PhD is no longer making you happy or fulfilled, sticking with it would amount to lot of time and energy spent on something that you don't enjoy. If you do decide not to continue, it's perfectly OK. A PhD is not for everyone and if it's not working for you, there is no shame in stepping away from it.

Chapter Five Takeaways

☐ Taking more time to finish your thesis as a result of a roadblock is by no means something to be embarrassed about. Staying the course in the face of roadblocks is actually something to be proud of and celebrated.

☐ Any departure from your initial research proposal is a natural part of pursuing a PhD. It's also an indication that your expertise and knowledge base are developing.

☐ While it is understandable that you'd want your project to be unique, the fact that others may be publishing on the same topic may not be as problematic as you think. It is also highly likely that, despite similarities, the way they've explored the topic will be distinct from your approach.

☐ Many people experience a certain degree of negative thinking in relation to themselves and their work. The trouble is that when a specific thought pattern is practiced over and over again, it starts to form a core belief system. In this respect, the biggest barrier to our progress is not something that comes from outside of us; it is actually our thinking that allows us to get in our own way.

☐ Sometimes we persist with things that aren't working because we are concerned about how it will look or what others will think of us. Pursuing a PhD is not for everyone and if it's no longer making you happy or fulfilled there is no shame in stepping away from it.

6

PUTTING YOUR IDEAS
(AND YOURSELF) OUT THERE

I don't feel ready to share my work

It's one thing to produce academic research and quite another to feel comfortable enough to put that work out into the world. If you tend to delay submitting drafts of your work and only do so when you are absolutely compelled to, you definitely aren't alone.

The thing about research is that there is always scope for revising it and, if we wanted to, we could spend the rest of our days continuously editing a single piece of work. However, this would not be a good use of our time, nor would it get us any closer to completing the PhD. The truth is that our work will probably never feel ready to share, no matter how much additional time we spend on it.

Typically, the reluctance to share work comes from an

underlying fear of how that work will be received. The prospect of others scrutinising our work can stir up feelings of vulnerability, especially when our work feels like a piece of ourselves. What if it provokes criticism or is deemed inadequate? What will people think of me if my work isn't good enough? These are the things that go through our minds when we hold onto our work too tightly.

The fear of scrutiny also reveals that we may be overidentifying with our research. No matter how personal our projects may feel to us or how much we may identify with what we are working on, we are not synonymous with our research. A PhD is something that we pursue and not fundamentally who we are.

The good news for doctoral students is that their ongoing research can be considered a work-in-progress. Our supervisors certainly aren't expecting us to submit polished work – if they did, they wouldn't have much of a role to play in supervising us. Therefore, the work we produce throughout the PhD is intended to be imperfect. Yet this is also precisely why our work requires engagement.

Research flourishes when it is shared, discussed, and even scrutinised by different audiences. This exposure enriches what we produce and helps to augment its quality. One of the most exciting things about producing research is to see others engaging with it. Were it just to sit on your computer and never see the light of day, it wouldn't have any impact at all. Only by bringing it out into the world does it have a chance to be influenced by others, and ultimately enhanced.

To help overcome some of the fears around sharing your work, I would suggest doing so in baby steps. For instance, you could begin by exchanging draft chapters with a colleague or friend – someone who you feel comfortable sharing it with. After generating some positive experiences with a person who feels safe, you can then start branching out to other peers to further build your confidence. Perhaps sharing your work on a conference panel or at a departmental seminar would be the next logical step. The more you practice sharing your research, the more you will come to see the value in that exchange. And hopefully, over time, any resistance around bringing your work out into the world will dissipate.

What if people steal my ideas?

Occasionally, the reluctance to share work does not stem from a fear of judgment, but rather, a fear that others may try to replicate our work in some way. If a PhD is intended to be our unique contribution to the field, it makes sense that we'd want to guard that work while the project is still in its infancy. After all, our contribution won't be very unique if someone runs away with our idea. Nevertheless, the likelihood of our work actually being 'stolen' by another person is highly unlikely. There are a number of reasons why we shouldn't be particularly concerned about this.

First, an important reality check. The truth is that no one generates research by remaining in a bubble, isolated from the world around them. At the end of the day, we are all influenced in one way or another by what we see, hear, or read from others. The same applies to your research, which has undoubtedly been affected by others in some shape or form. This is an important point to bear in mind whenever we start to feel territorial about our research area.

I've heard several doctoral students admit that one of their least favourite parts of being in a PhD programme is the competitive atmosphere between themselves and their peers. Being overly cagey about your work, out of fear that someone may steal your ideas, runs the risk of intensifying a competitive atmosphere between you and your fellow students. It suggests that you have little trust in those around you and are therefore unwilling to converse about your research.

Even if we assume the worst, that someone has decided to replicate your entire project, it is virtually impossible that they would even be able to. Take two people with the exact same topic, and perhaps even the same overarching argument, and they would most likely end up submitting two very different pieces of work. This highlights even more why the fear about someone stealing your ideas is unnecessary and unfounded.

Putting our work out into the world is at the heart of what academics do. Receiving feedback from different audiences is ultimately what strengthens research. By refusing to share your work out of fear, you end up more isolated than you need to be and also forgo the benefits of engaging others in your work. In short, there is much more to lose in being overly protective of your research than there is to gain.

I'm nervous about an upcoming presentation

Few people actually enjoy standing up in front of an audience and speaking. Whether it's a seminar presentation, a lecture, delivering a conference paper, or even the simple act of introducing yourself to a group of strangers, public speaking can feel like an immensely daunting undertaking.

Studies have shown that some people rate their fear of public speaking over their fear of death.[10] What that means is that if these people had to attend a funeral, they would prefer to be the one in the coffin instead of having to deliver the eulogy! The resistance to public speaking could not be more severe.

Those who feel anxious when presenting will recall some of the physical sensations they tend to experience when they are in front of an audience. This may include having their heart race, a shortness of breath, blushing, sweating, dry mouth, nausea and even shaking.

What these physical sensations reveal is the body's fight-versus-flight response system being activated.

The fight-versus-flight response is our body's automatic physiological response to something we perceive as life threatening.[11] Although the activation of this system is useful when we are faced with a genuine threat to life, as the experience of public speaking demonstrates, fight-versus-flight can also be activated in situations that fall short of that level of danger. It is, rather, the perception of danger that has built up in our minds that facilitates fight-versus-flight in such situations. We don't often acknowledge the power of our thoughts and how our mind impacts the body, however, working through this piece of the puzzle is the single most important factor in overcoming presentation anxiety.

If presenting is not actually life threatening, yet our body is perceiving it to be dangerous, we need to find a way to shift our perception. Since our mind is not likely to shift overnight, we need to begin by making the shift within our body first. The key to doing this is to consciously slow ourselves down. Slowing yourself down in the midst of a presentation may seem counterintuitive.

If you happen to be nervous, your instincts will likely encourage you to do the exact opposite – to speed up. However, the simple action of slowing down unlocks one of the quickest stress-busters that we have access to in any given moment, and that is our breathing.

By consciously controlling your breathing through taking steady, slow breaths, you can instantly de-activate the fight-versus-flight response system and, in turn, minimize the uncomfortable symptoms that may arise during a presentation. This simple but effective tool is a crucial first step in breaking the cycle of presentation anxiety. If you find yourself struggling to slow down the pace of your presentation, try the following strategies:

✓ Ask rhetorical questions throughout

✓ Take pauses or repeat key words for emphasis

✓ Show relevant YouTube clips to give yourself a break from speaking

✓ Show images or graphics

✓ Refer to a slide pack or a handout

✓ Use a whiteboard

✓ Engage the audience by taking a quick poll or survey

✓ Ask the audience to briefly converse with their neighbours on a specific topic

✓ Take sips of water during the presentation

For further guidance on steps to alleviate presentation anxiety visit the *Doctoral De-Stress* Book Bonuses page on academease.org.

How do I handle a challenging Q&A session?

For many students the most dreaded aspect of an academic presentation is not the presentation itself, but the question and answer (Q&A) session that follows it. Q&As are not only unpredictable, they are also tough to prepare for. We can never be sure what we are going to be asked and by whom. It is no wonder that the prospect of a Q&A session is unsettling for many.

Much of the fear surrounding Q&A sessions stems from the feeling of being on the spot or under attack. Instead of thinking of it as an attack, try and view it as more of a conversation with your audience.

Before you respond to any questions during a Q&A, pause and take a slow, deep breath. As noted in the previous section, it is not uncommon to speed up during both the presentation and the Q&A. However, the faster we go, the more we yield to the fight-versus-flight stress response mechanism. Our fight-versus-flight response is governed by our more primitive, reptilian brain – the part of our mind that is concerned with our survival above all else. In such a state, we are unlikely to be able to access the sophisticated and creative thinking associated with the more advanced part of the human brain – our neo-cortex.[12] Yet, this is precisely the part of our brain that we want to have access to during the Q&A.

When answering questions, remember that not all questions in a Q&A session are created equal; in fact, some are downright unfair. If, for example, an audience member goes on a rant for a considerable period of time – as almost always happen at some point during a Q&A – it is worth asking if there is a question in what they have said or if it was more of a comment. In other words, it's perfectly reasonable to question the question. By doing so, you are inviting them to either reframe their question or retract it.

On a related note, remember that it's not your job to interpret a poorly phrased question. Before you attempt to offer a response, ensure that you have understood the question clearly. If anything is unclear, don't hesitate to ask the questioner for clarification. One way to do this would be to restate the question as you have heard it and then ask the questioner to confirm if you have understood it correctly. Or you could simply ask the questioner to be clearer in how they've formulated their question.

Perhaps our greatest fear during a Q&A is that we will be asked something that we don't know. The most common approach to this type of scenario is to either pretend we do know, or to provide an answer to the question we wish we had been asked. Neither of these approaches feels particularly authentic. However, what if not every Q required an A? If we assumed that were true, we could instead say something along the lines of: 'I don't know the answer to that, but it's a really interesting question. I'll have to give it some more thought.' While some may be reluctant to admit that they don't have all the answers, out of fear they might look stupid, in my view it signifies the exact opposite – a person who is confident enough in themselves and in their work to admit that they don't have all the answers.

Finally, although it may feel redundant to you, it may be worth repeating material from your presentation during the Q&A. The audience will not be as familiar with the material in your presentation. An additional benefit of referring back to your presentation script is that it equips you with a ready-made response. This can only help in building your confidence throughout the Q&A session. As

I've often found that one confident response leads to another and another, and so on.

For a downloadable summary of tips for navigating an academic Q&A visit the *Doctoral De-Stress* Book Bonuses page on academease.org.

What's the best way to deal with negative feedback?

Compliments can be hard to come by in the academic arena. This is particularly the case for PhD students. Negative feedback can come from a variety of differently places – your supervisor, colleagues and peers, or other faculty members in your department.

Endless criticism can feel exhausting and become a major de-motivator. It can also be difficult not to take the criticism personally, particularly if you are used to excelling academically, as many doctoral students are. What, then, is the best way to cope with negative feedback?

The first thing is to simply realize that the criticism of your project is normal and even to be expected. While you may have grown accustomed to receiving compliments on your work, it's important to appreciate that the PhD is an entirely different ball game and, by its very nature, subject to a higher level of scrutiny. So as strange as it may sound, it is actually an indication of the more demanding level you are working at.

Since a higher amount of negative feedback is to be expected during the PhD, it's also important to understand that it's meant to help you. It may feel awful in the moment, but whenever I ask a student to reflect on the criticism they receive, they almost always acknowledge that it will make their project better in the longer-term. The key question to ask yourself is – is this criticism constructive? If the answer is yes, try viewing the criticism as an opportunity to improve your project.

When the criticism isn't particularly constructive or delivered in a respectful manner, remember that it usually says more about the person delivering the criticism than you. Not all pieces of feedback need to be taken on board. Part of reflecting on the feedback surrounding your work is to decide which comments you want to accept and which ones to disregard.

The next point to consider is that the PhD is what you are doing and not who you are. With that in mind, try your best not to overidentify with your research or to take criticism of it personally. This can be challenging, as our projects are often deeply personal to us, but at the end of the day, the criticism of your work isn't an attack on you or a reflection of your worth.

If you are feeling weighed down by the volume of criticism you have received and are starting to seriously question the value of your project, don't hesitate to request more positive feedback. This could be something along the lines of: 'Thanks for your helpful feedback. I now have a sense of what the gaps are and what can be improved. To make sure I'm on the right track, it would be great to hear what aspects of the project you think are promising.'

Finally, rather than seeking approval externally, remember that the main person who really needs to buy into your project is not your supervisor, your colleagues or anyone else – it's you. What you think matters more than anyone else. Instead of waiting to hear from others that you are doing OK, start to give yourself the validation you are seeking externally by keeping track of what is going well. Begin writing these things down and come back to the list whenever you need a boost.

Chapter Six Takeaways

☐ Research flourishes when it is shared, discussed and even scrutinised by different audiences. This exposure enriches what we produce and helps to augment its quality. As such, there is much more to lose by being overly protective of your research than there is to gain.

☐ If presenting is not actually life-threatening, yet our body is perceiving it to be a dangerous activity, we need to find a way to alleviate the physiological symptoms of presentation anxiety. A useful starting point is to consciously slow yourself down.

☐ Remember that not all questions in a Q&A session are created equal. It's perfectly reasonable to question the question and to admit what you don't know. For further guidance on Q&A sessions and academic presentations visit the *Doctoral De-Stress* Book Bonuses page on academease.org.

☐ Not all pieces of feedback need to be taken on board. Part of navigating the feedback surrounding your work is to decide which comments you want to accept and which ones to disregard.

☐ Rather than seeking approval externally, the main person who really needs to buy into your project is not your supervisor, your colleagues or anyone else – it's you. Instead of waiting to hear from others that you are doing OK, start to give yourself the validation you are seeking externally.

7

THE BALANCING ACT: JUGGLING THE PHD WITH OTHER COMMITMENTS

I feel too busy to work on my PhD

As if the demands of completing a PhD were not enough to have on your plate, nowadays there is pressure for students to go beyond submitting their doctorate. In addition to conducting independent and original research, students are now expected to attend conferences, acquire teaching experience, apply for postdoc positions, and publish in high-quality academic journals, and the list could go on. It no longer feels like enough to solely work towards the PhD, particularly among those who have in mind an academic career. Today's doctorate is essentially a PhD Plus.

Given the pressure to pursue a PhD Plus, I've met

many students that work on these supplementary pursuits at the expense of their research. It can even get to the point where they no longer have the time to progress with their PhD work. Building up their academic portfolio with a list of publications seems to be a matter of greater urgency than completing the PhD itself.

While it is undeniably important to augment the PhD experience, it's essential to keep the various tasks in front of you in perspective. Your research should still be the central component of what you are working towards. The PhD is the cake and everything else – while admittedly important – is the icing on that cake. The icing can't exist in isolation of the cake and it certainly doesn't carry the same weight. In other words, there is a natural hierarchy to the tasks you pursue during a PhD and your research must take precedence above these other endeavours.

Sometimes chasing these supplemental items can not only come at the expense of your work, but your general happiness as well. It encourages students to lose sight of what an accomplishment it is to obtain a PhD. So much of the 'icing' that students chase after is never-ending, as there could always be more publications to secure, more conferences to attend, and more funding to apply for. This is perhaps why I've noticed increasing numbers of students who, despite completing their PhDs, end up feeling like they could have done more.

By all means, focus on augmenting your PhD experience, particularly if you do want an academic career. However, never lose sight of what an impressive achievement it is to obtain a PhD. It has always been, and remains, a huge accomplishment that is significantly watered down by the expectation to be doing everything else alongside it.

How do I balance the PhD with my teaching commitments?

Most doctoral students will have an opportunity to gain some teaching experience during their PhD. Although the type of teaching experience on offer will vary by department, it will likely involve serving as a Graduate Teaching Assistant (GTA) for undergraduate students at your university. The teaching duties for a GTA range from marking assignments, holding office hours and leading classroom seminars to delivering lectures.

One thing I've observed about the GTA role is how little training is available to help doctoral students prepare themselves to teach. The lack of training offered to doctoral students is surprising when you consider that none of them will have had any prior teaching experience. They are simply expected to dive in and automatically know how to teach a group of undergraduates. In my own experience, I remember being offered only a few hours of training before being thrown into the classroom. I'll never forget how nervous I was on my first day and how ill-prepared I felt.

Aside from the absence of teacher training, I recall there being very little advice for how to effectively balance teaching commitments with pursuing a PhD. If, however, doctoral students are expected to juggle teaching and research, it seems imperative to discuss some techniques for this. Whether it's one class or multiple classes, the time that you put into teaching can easily eat away your research time, which is why it is essential to establish some boundaries between the two. Below are a few tips to better balance your teaching responsibilities with the PhD.

Preparation: Teaching preparation can feel like a never-ending task. There will always be one more article you could read prior to a class. I've found that the preparation tends to expand to fill whatever time you have available and, as such, can easily turn into a full-time job. Although it's understandable that you'd want to spend as much time as possible on teaching prep, particularly if you are new to teaching, it's important to set some limits on the time you spend preparing. Try compartmentalising your preparation into 1-2 days per week, as close to the day you are teaching as possible so everything is fresh in your mind. Then allow yourself to focus on your research during the remaining days.

Part of the reason why we over-prepare is because we want to appear to be an expert. Chances are, however, that you are going to have to teach many topics outside of your comfort zone in which you are by no means an expert. Instead of feeling like you need to have all the answers, above all you want to encourage your students to discuss and engage with the material. This may require playing around with the structure of your classes in order to facilitate participation among the students. It could involve role playing, class debates, simulations, and other activities. I remember how much more enjoyable teaching became for me, and my students, when I stopped expecting myself to be an expert on every topic and started to alter the format of each class in order to maximise their participation.

Availability: Although I remember a time without smartphones and email, the majority of today's undergraduate students do not. They have grown accustomed to electronic communication and instant responses. It is therefore more likely than not that you'll receive emails from your students outside of regular working hours. Since many of us are now used to operating in this way, you may feel compelled to respond to emails from students irrespective of the time of day or whether it's a weekend. However, I would strongly advise against engaging with emails outside of working hours. For one, it creates an expectation that you are always available and precludes you from having any downtime. By not responding right away, you can teach your students when you are available and when you are not. I recommend having two set windows of email availability throughout the day in order to scan and respond to emails from students. Spend no more than 15-20 minutes during each window to ensure it doesn't take longer than it needs to.

Requests: In addition to your regular teaching responsibilities, you may also be approached by your students for other requests, whether it's a last-minute reference letter request or an extension on their assignment. It can be helpful to have some policies decided on in advance in order to manage incoming requests. On the former, you shouldn't feel compelled to write a reference letter for every student that requests one. You can kindly redirect them to someone more appropriate or mention that you will only write references at the end of the academic year. If you are happy to write a reference, your policy could be that you require a minimum of two-week's notice in order to discourage last minute requests. What you don't want is to feel compelled to write references on someone else's timescale. In these situations, you are within your rights to say no.

In terms of extensions, you can be sure that students will ask for them for a variety of reasons. It's up to you to determine what constitutes a reasonable request. In my view, having multiple, competing deadlines is not a valid excuse for requesting an extension. Since students will know in advance when assignments are due it is up to them to plan accordingly. You aren't doing your students, or yourself, any favours by agreeing to any and all extension requests. In order to respect your time, which would otherwise be spent marking late assignments, have some general guidelines in place and communicate them to your students during your first class. It also helps to reiterate them in a follow-up email so no one can claim ignorance with regards to the guidelines. Having some policies decided on in advance provides an opportunity to establish some boundaries early on with your students.

Feedback: The prospect of having your teaching evaluated can be nerve-racking. Anyone who has taught will know how challenging it is to garner entirely positive feedback across the board. Even if your teaching term has gone very well and your classes adore you, there tends to be at least one person (and hopefully just the one!) who only has negative comments. It's tough not to take such comments to heart. Although it may be an outlier, it's natural to focus on that one negative comment, even at the expense of countless positive comments. If it is just the odd comment, it's best to try and let it go. The student may have an axe to grind and could be taking it out on you.

What you will want to look out for with student feedback are any patterns. For instance, if multiple students have made the same type of comment, and not just a single disgruntled student, it's worth reflecting on. Like any skill, teaching requires practice and there is always scope for improvement. Student feedback can be a great opportunity to enhance or improve your teaching, as long as you can approach it constructively and not beat yourself up about it.

As mentioned above, there is very little training offered to doctoral students who are new to teaching, so the fact that you may encounter a few bumps in your teaching is to be expected. In my own experience, I only learned what worked well in my teaching practice by first experiencing what didn't work so well.

I'm nervous about finding a job

Applying for jobs in the midst of completing your PhD can feel very overwhelming. Students are frequently told how competitive the job market is, which can create a lot of fear and panic. As early as their first year, I see students starting to worry about their job prospects post-PhD. When left unchecked, this fear can become all-consuming and start to impede progress on the PhD itself. Instead of working on your thesis, you may find yourself repeatedly checking job adverts or allowing your mind to wander back to this topic.

The search for a job may also foster a no-win comparison between yourself and others. Whether it's one of your peers who has been successful on the job market leaving you feeling bad about your prospects; or someone who has come across obstacles in their job search, thereby constituting proof for you of how tough it is to find a job. Whichever way you look at it, there doesn't seem to be much good news on the job search front when drawing from others' experiences. When we are faced with uncertainty over something like this, we often invent stories about our job prospects. All of which seem to further intensify anxiety and worry about finding a job.

Given all of this, what's the best way to handle a job

search in the middle of your PhD? Ideally, you want to explore the opportunities that are available in a manner that causes minimal disruption to your work. You also want to find a way for it to only occupy a limited amount of your time and headspace. My advice to students who are in the process of searching for jobs is to begin by setting aside one hour, once per week. If you are spending longer than this on your search, on multiple days each week, you may want to consider whether this additional time is serving you well.

After you've set aside the time for your search, I recommend finding a space where you don't tend to do your PhD work, a café in your neighbourhood or near your university for instance. Bring along a journal or notebook that is specifically dedicated to your search. For the one hour you have set aside, do nothing else but a broad search of opportunities from the main job advert sites. You can make the task feel lighter by listening to some music and enjoying a cup of coffee during that time. Note down any relevant jobs that you come across, along with the application deadlines. Try to minimize any pressure on yourself by treating it as an exploratory exercise. You are simply scanning various opportunities that are out there. When the hour is up, close your job search journal and leave the space.

Having a specific time carved out, and conducting your search in a separate space to your normal working environment helps to establish some important boundaries with a task that might otherwise occupy much more of your time. It also allows you to get excited about the possibility of finding a job, while limiting the time you have available to ruminate or worry. If you find yourself worrying about jobs outside of this time, remind yourself that you have a dedicated window to focus on the task.

This helps to protect your time and keep you focused on your PhD work.

If you are starting to think about applying for jobs, try this technique for the next few weeks and see if it helps make the job search feel more manageable. Once you've narrowed down a few prospective jobs to apply for, here are a few additional tips to keep in mind:

- When you find a position that you'd like to apply for, try not to become overly attached to it. The best way to do this is to zoom out and allow yourself to see that there are other possibilities beyond that one job. If you think you need something in order to be happy, it's a sign you are overly attached to it.

- Give up the mentality of lack and scarcity – the idea that there aren't enough jobs to go around. While this mindset is very common in academia, it breeds a lot of anxiety and puts unnecessary pressure on you.

- When you apply for something, give it your best shot but remember that you only control 50% of the process. The other 50% is beyond your control, as there may be factors behind the scenes that you aren't even aware of. All you can do is work on your half of the equation, putting together the strongest application possible, and then letting go of trying to control the other half.

- Despite the image that most people project of themselves, it takes time to land the ideal job. Even the strongest candidates will encounter their fair share of rejection letters over time. Instead of setting unrealistic expectations for yourself and comparing yourself to others, remind yourself that patience is a virtue when it comes to job applications.

- Getting to the interview stage is a success in its own right and should be celebrated. If you ever feel like you screwed up an interview or an application, remember that this is a learning process. Interview skills are something you can improve, so try to treat the experience as an opportunity to develop.

- Whatever setbacks you encounter in applying for jobs, these do not need to define you unless you allow them to. If things don't work out as you hoped in relation to a specific job, remember that there could be something better out there for you.

I don't have time for any hobbies

The previous sections in this chapter have dealt with how to juggle the many pressures on a PhD student's plate. Given that most PhD plates are overflowing, the emphasis has been on boundary setting and learning to say no to what isn't essential, with a view to prioritising your PhD work. There is one item for which the opposite holds true, wherein you would actually benefit from adding to your plate, and that is a hobby.

Interestingly, hobbies are an area in which a lot of doctoral students are able to say no with relative ease. If they are already struggling to minimise the commitments on their plates, it would seem to make sense to put their hobbies on hold until after they've submitted. Spending time on a hobby in the middle of their PhDs may feel like a luxury that they simply cannot afford.

Unlike all of the other things that may be crowding

your plate, hobbies are in a different category altogether and there are a number of reasons for this. First, when you do something you truly enjoy, it doesn't deplete your time and energy in the way that other tasks do. A hobby actually gives something back to you. It recharges you and makes you feel energised. The idea that pursuing a hobby will compete with, or come at the expense of, your research time is simply not true. By providing you with an outlet to properly detach from your research, something that many students struggle to do, it can actually enhance your work.

Moreover, pursuing a hobby for the pure joy of it – whether it's dancing, painting, playing racquetball, or swimming – reminds you of who you are outside of your PhD project. Although many students tend to identify with their work, at some point you won't be a PhD student anymore. Having a pastime is a powerful reminder that life exists beyond the PhD bubble.

Finally, pursuing a hobby can be beneficial because you don't necessarily need to be the best at it. This can be quite a refreshing change from your academic work, whereby you may feel considerable pressure to be at the top of your field.

Notwithstanding the many advantages associated with adding a hobby to your PhD plate, there may still be a lot of resistance to it. If that's the case, try it on a trial basis for a few weeks and see whether it makes a difference to how you feel and how you approach your work. If you aren't sure where to start, begin by making a list of any extra-curricular activities that you enjoy or have been meaning to try. Look up what classes are available in your area. Dedicate 30 minutes to 1 hour per week to one of the activities you have identified and commit to doing it regularly. If that's not possible, try doing something on a monthly basis and see how you feel.

When you consider the benefits referred to above, it's actually not a question of whether you can afford to spend time on a hobby. It's more a question of whether you can afford not to.

My friends and family aren't supportive of my PhD

Pursuing a PhD can be a very isolating experience. Unless you are part of a collaborative research team, you are most likely toiling away on your own, day in and day out. Even if you tend to view working independently as one of the perks of PhD life, it can nevertheless feel quite lonely at times.

The extent to which our friends and families support us on our PhD journey can either mitigate or further intensify these feelings of isolation. In reality, your friends and family may have very little clue about the content of your PhD project. Given how much of ourselves we devote to our research, it may feel like an oversight if those closest to us don't seem that interested or supportive of our work. What's worse is that our nearest and dearest may resent the time we have to put into our research, particularly if it comes at the expense of our time with them.

The fact that we may not discuss our PhD work at length with our loved ones is not that uncommon, nor is it necessarily a bad thing. If we already have colleagues and supervisors to discuss our work with, we may not need our friends and family to be able to converse with us about the intricacies of our work. It can actually be quite refreshing to spend time with people who don't care how many chapters we've written or what methodology we are using. Our family and friends may be a great tonic to the stresses of a PhD by keeping us grounded, present and generally less stuck in our academic ivory towers.

That being said, it's natural to want the support of our family and friends, but we may need to shift our expectations of what form that support takes. At a minimum we want those closest to us to know our general area of research, to happily cheer us on from the side-lines, to remind us what is important when we hit a bump in the road and to celebrate the milestones we achieve on our PhD journey.

Unfortunately, a lack of support can show up in a much more aggressive way. For instance, a friend or family member may belittle our work or make inappropriate comments about our PhD. This could be something along the lines of: 'You are so lucky you don't have to go to work'; 'Students are lazy'; 'Why is it taking you so long to finish your PhD?'; 'Who's going to bother reading your thesis anyways?' Not only are these comments unsupportive and judgmental, they demonstrate ignorance about what a PhD entails. While there are many reasons why a person might make such remarks, the crucial thing to keep in mind is that their comments have very little to do with you.

People who attack and belittle in this way only do so from a place of insecurity. A person who is truly happy in themselves does not lash out or make judgements about others. Getting a PhD is no small feat and for whatever reason, something about it may be threatening to them. Whatever the underlying cause of their behaviour might be, it's not your responsibility to figure it out.

As much as you may want to convince a family member or a friend that your work has merit, it'll likely be a wasted effort. In such situations, it's best to accept that you won't receive their support and move on. This might be a hugely disappointing realisation, particularly if it is someone close to you, but you don't need everyone in the world to approve of you, praise you, or to see value in your work. At the end of the day, the only person you should be doing your PhD for is you.

Chapter Seven Takeaways

☐ While your PhD plate may be filled up with other commitments (e.g. teaching, publishing, searching for a job and attending conferences), your actual PhD research should take precedence above all other activities.

☐ While it is useful to gain some teaching experience, it is important to balance your teaching responsibilities with your PhD research. This will involve paying particular attention to teaching preparation, your general availability to students, and strategies for handling additional requests that you receive.

☐ Searching and applying for jobs can be a full-time job in itself. Having a separate space from your normal working environment, as well as a specific time to conduct your search each week, will help to establish some important boundaries. It also allows you to get excited about the possibility of finding a job, while limiting the time you have available to ruminate or worry.

☐ Although many students tend to over-identify with

their work, at some point you won't be a PhD student anymore. Having a pastime or hobby is a powerful reminder that life exists beyond your PhD.

☐ It's natural to want the support of family and friends throughout the PhD, but we may need to shift our expectations of what form that support takes. At a minimum we want those closest to us to know our general area of research, to happily cheer us on from the side-lines, to remind us what is important when we hit a bump in the road and to celebrate the milestones we achieve on our PhD journey.

8

DEFENDING YOUR WORK: NAVIGATING THE VIVA PROCESS

How does a viva differ from a regular academic presentation?

You've reached a significant milestone and submitted your thesis, but now there is one final hurdle awaiting you – the viva. So much of the viva seems to be shrouded in mystery. Many students walk into it not quite knowing what to expect or how the process works. This can make the entire exercise even more nerve-racking. In this chapter I'll address certain aspects of the viva, but I want to start off by demystifying the viva process itself.

The term 'viva' is short for *viva voce*, meaning oral examination in Latin. It's an opportunity for your examiners to discuss your work and ask you questions, while also ensuring that you are the author of the submitted thesis.

At some universities the term 'defence' is used inter-changeably with 'viva' and I have to admit that I'm not a fan of using this term. While there may be some truth to it insofar as the viva is an opportunity to defend your pro-ject – there is also something profoundly unhelpful and counterproductive about this language, as it puts stu-dents into defensive mode. The implication of referring to the examination as a defence is that the examiners will be aggressive and on the offensive. They will attack your work and the best way to prepare yourself is to put on your armour and get ready to fight back.

Approaching the examination as a defence of your work not only puts you into fight-versus-flight mode as you prepare, the feeling of being under attack may also inhibit your performance. Instead of approaching your viva in a fear-based way, my advice is to reframe it as more of a conversation about your project. This will help release some of the pressure surrounding the viva and allow you to tap into what first inspired you about your research area.

A conversation does not have to be unpleasant or un-comfortable, and in fact, it can even be enjoyable. It is also a more accurate description of what the viva actually entails. In contrast to an academic presentation, where you would typically give a brief summary of your work, you won't be expected to give an overview of your re-search. When you show up to the viva, it is assumed that your examiners will have thoroughly read your work, and they will jump straight into the discussion.

In the UK, there are typically two examiners at each viva. One tends to be drawn from within the student's home department whereas the second is an external person, from another academic institution. You will have some choice in selecting your examiners as you near completion. Your supervisor may have some ideas for appropriate examiners, but you can also suggest individuals if you already have some in mind. As a rule, supervisors don't usually attend their students' vivas, and on the rare occasions that they do, they are expected to refrain from speaking throughout.

One of the most difficult things to predict is how long your viva will last. The truth is that the length of a viva really varies – some are as short as an hour whereas others are several hours long. It's also difficult to attribute any meaning to the length of time, as it's not always the case that a very long viva is indicative of any problems with the thesis. It could be that the examiners are genuinely interested in the topic and have a lot to discuss with the student. Equally, we can't assume anything if the viva is relatively short.

The results of the viva tend to be announced to a student on the day. You may first be asked to leave the room while the examiners confer with one another before announcing the result. Whatever the outcome, the examiners will follow-up by compiling their comments in a report. The report will provide an overview of the viva and the result, along with any corrections you have been requested to make.

Perhaps what makes the viva process so mysterious is that each student's experience tends to vary significantly. It really comes down to the individuals involved and how they interact with your work. It is precisely because of this variance that you should take others' experiences with a pinch of salt. No two people will have an entirely similar viva. Despite whatever stories you hear from others about their viva, it's best to remember that your experience will be your own.

Is there any way that I can prepare for my viva?

The uncertainty surrounding the viva process can often leave students stumped over how to prepare. Although it's impossible to predict how things will go on the day or what the examiners' assessment of your thesis will be, there are a number of things you can do to put yourself in the best position possible. Below are the main steps I would recommend in advance of your viva:

- Read through your thesis to refresh your memory. In particular, you want to make a note of – and be able to speak about – the following items: your central argument; the contribution your work makes; how your research fits within the literature; an explanation of your methodology; and finally, any avenues for future research that your project opens up.

- Get to know your examiners. It's important to know the individuals you will be dealing with on the day, so do a bit of background research that goes beyond scanning their bios. Who are they and how are they likely to view your work given their particular perspective and background?

- Try and brainstorm some possible questions you may be asked and practice answering them. Although you won't be able to anticipate everything in advance, it will give you some practice in fielding questions.

- Are there any gaps in your research? Try to think about what some of the potential limitations of your research are. Could you reframe these limitations as avenues for further research?

- Arrange for a mock viva with your supervisor or another colleague. Try to do this at least a week or two weeks before the viva to give you enough time to prepare and reflect on how it went.

- As mentioned in the previous section, reframing the viva as a conversation (instead of a defence) will allow you to show up differently on the day. It will influence how you carry yourself, how you respond to questions and, ultimately, how much you are able to get out of the experience. The conversation is there to improve the project and ultimately help you – so there's no need to feel under attack.

- Dress for the occasion. Rather than picking something standard from your wardrobe for the day, spend some time selecting an outfit. Not only will dressing for the occasion help you exude confidence, it will convey a sense of professionalism to your examiners. If it isn't feasible for you to buy a new outfit, little flourishes can also go a long way towards boosting your confidence.

- As strange as it may sound, try and get excited about the viva. In other words, don't lose sight of what you find exciting and enjoyable about the project. Tapping into your excitement is one of the best antidotes to fear and anxiety. Given that you dedicated so much of your time to working on your PhD, the opportunity to have colleagues engage with your work is actually something to look forward to and to be excited about.

For a downloadable viva prep checklist visit the *Doctoral De-Stress* Book Bonuses page on academease.org.

How do I manage difficult questions from the examiners?

No matter how well we prepare ourselves for the viva, there is no way to actually anticipate what questions we may be asked. So how can we manage challenging questions, particularly the pesky ones we may not have answers to?

Given that you are being assessed on a piece of work that you have spent years researching, the chances of you having no response to a question is unlikely. Nevertheless, I do recall in a number of situations feeling stumped in the moment, only to have the perfect response to a question come into my mind hours after the fact. What this means is that I had the answer somewhere in my mind all along, but my nerves didn't allow me to access it.

As with regular presentations and Q&As, when we are nervous we slip into fight-versus-flight mode and our primitive brain takes over. The more at ease we feel during the viva, the better placed we'll be to respond to questions with confidence. Here are a few things to try in order to put yourself at ease.

The first thing I would suggest is to take notes during the viva. It's not at all unusual to want a record of the conversation with your examiners, and it's not something they are likely to object to. In addition to having a record of what was said for your own reference, the act of taking notes can give you that essential space between being asked a question and having to give an answer. In that moment you can pause, take a breath and collect your thoughts before responding. By doing this you won't have to feel as though you are on the spot.

Putting yourself in a state of ease also comes down to

your perspective. If the viva really is more of a conversation than an attack, it isn't the case that you'll be standing in front of a firing squad on the day. A conversation is not one-sided and, as such, there is always scope for you to question the question. If something doesn't make sense to you, you can ask for clarity. If a question seems off topic, you can redirect the examiners back to what is relevant. And if you perceive a question to be unfair, you are within your rights to throw it back to the examiners.

I also remind students to refer back to parts of their thesis as much as possible during the viva. There may be some reluctance to do this given that the examiners have already read the thesis in full. However, reading it through once does not make them an expert on your thesis. They may be an expert in the field, but you are the real expert on your project and no one will be as familiar with the details as you.

It is also important to bear in mind that the examiners may not have the same background knowledge as you. Therefore, things that you feel are obvious may by no means be obvious to them. Here is where a bit of research into your examiners' backgrounds – one of the tips mentioned in the previous section – may help you determine what level of detail to provide in your explanations and responses to certain questions.

For many, the weight surrounding the viva has a lot to do with their expectation that a doctoral thesis should be perfect. After all, this is the culmination of years of research and endless hours of work. Nevertheless, as you approach your viva, it's important to remind yourself that the thesis is not intended to be a perfect, ready-to-publish piece of work. There will be imperfections in it and that's OK. Try your best not to be thrown off by difficult questions, criticisms or challenges to your work.

Take the pressure off and think of the viva as an opportunity to get useful feedback in order to further enhance your project.

What if I fail my viva?

The prospect of failing the viva is a very real fear for a lot of students, yet the statistics reveal that this fear is largely unfounded. It is actually rare for a student to make it all the way to the final stage of their PhD and end up failing.

The viva is by no means the first opportunity to have your work assessed during the PhD. Most programmes will have some mechanism to assess a student's work at key points throughout the PhD. Whether it's comprehensive exams, termly assessments, upgrade panels or a transfer viva, every institution or department will have such mechanisms in place to confirm that students are on track.

Aside from trusting the PhD process at your institution, it is also important to have some faith in your supervisor. Irrespective of what your relationship has been with them – positive or negative – it is unlikely they will allow you to reach the viva stage if failure is likely. Remember, their reputation is on the line as much as yours is and, in that sense, they have an incentive to ensure you only sit the viva when you are ready.

Even if we were to assume the worst and the viva goes horribly wrong, in all likelihood you would have an opportunity to re-sit the viva before receiving an outright fail. In this way, the system that is in place is actually there to support you and facilitate you passing. In other words, a lot would have to go wrong in order for you to fail the viva process completely.

The real question, therefore, is not whether you will pass or fail, it is the extent of revisions you will receive when you do pass. The quantity of your revisions can range from major corrections to passing with no corrections at all. Having the examiners request major revisions can be disappointing, particularly if you were keen to close the PhD chapter of your life and swiftly move on to something else, but it's not a bad result at all. The examiners' reports will most likely be fairly detailed about what changes are required and the amount of time you have to complete the revisions.

Although it's natural to fear the worst, try and remove the fear of failure as a possibility in your mind. Worry and fear take up a great deal of energy and, in the end, both accomplish very little. Removing the prospect of failure as a possibility will hopefully free up some mental space and allow you to face your viva with confidence.

I passed my viva but don't feel as excited as I expected

You've submitted your thesis, passed your viva, and now you find yourself on the other side of the finish line. There is so much to celebrate in what you've achieved. Although you should feel on top of the world, for whatever reason you don't. In fact, you feel the opposite. Low, unsettled, empty and somewhat unanchored. After hearing countless students describe these feelings, and having experienced it to a certain degree myself, I've dubbed this unexpected confluence of emotions as the 'Post-PhD blues.'

Some of the feelings that arise during the post-PhD period may be related to the viva itself. Despite passing and perhaps having few or no corrections at all, you may nevertheless feel disappointed with how it went. Parts of it may have felt a bit underwhelming and anti-climactic. You may also have the sense that your examiners did not fully engage with your work in the way that you would have liked. Moreover, even if the viva did go well, it may feel somewhat strange to have years of your life and all your hard work condensed into just a few hours. The time devoted to the assessment hardly seems to do justice to all the sacrifice and commitment that went into producing your thesis.

There may also be a sense of loss in reaching the culmination of your PhD journey. As much as you may have yearned to reach this milestone, pursuing a PhD has been a part of your life for so long, and even a part of your identity. You may not have a sense of who you are in the absence of this project and that can be a little unsettling.

Whatever the underlying causes of your post-PhD blues are, try and be as gentle with yourself as possible. Life after the PhD is a huge transition and will require some adjustment. A few simple things can make a world of difference:

1. **Focus on Beginnings:** First, try something new. Beginning something can be a powerful way to help you mark this new phase in your life and make peace with the phase that has just ended.

2. **Take a Break:** If you haven't got your next step figured out just yet, try not to let this uncertainty detract from the incredible achievement of passing your viva. You will figure out the next step in time. Not having something lined up immediately is a good excuse to give yourself a well-deserved break.

3. **Treat Yourself:** This is the time to treat yourself to something. It could be something that you've been

putting off doing until you finished, or something you'd like to buy yourself to celebrate your achievement. It doesn't matter what this item or activity is – whether it's big, small, expensive or cheap – as long as it has some significance for you.

4. **Enjoy Simple Pleasures:** Take time to enjoy the little things – for instance, all of the things you couldn't do while you were working on your thesis. Like waking up late, taking time to go for a long walk or enjoying a coffee, all without feeling any pressure to rush back to your desk to write. You now have the freedom to do anything, so enjoy it!

I firmly believe that a lot of the melancholy following a PhD comes from viewing it as the end of a long journey. While in some respects it is, it's also the beginning of another journey. If you decide to stay in academia, it'll be the first of many research projects. Likewise, if you decide to go on and do something different, it'll be the first step on this new path. Even if you end up going in a completely unrelated direction, you will have learned a valuable set of life skills during the PhD that you can draw upon as you go forward. Whichever way you look at it, passing the final stage of your PhD is just the beginning.

Chapter Eight Takeaways

☐ Instead of approaching the *viva voce* as a defence of your work, try to reframe it as more of a conversation. This subtle shift will diffuse some of the pressure surrounding the viva and allow you to tap into what first inspired you about your research area.

☐ Although it's impossible to predict how things will

go on the day or what the examiners' assessment of your thesis will be, there are a number of things you can do to put yourself in the best position possible. Prior to your viva, you should read through your thesis and make a note of the following: your central argument; the contribution your work makes; how your research fits within the literature; an explanation of your methodology; and finally, any avenues for future research that your project opens up. As a further aid, download the checklist for viva prep from the *Doctoral De-Stress* Book Bonuses page on academease.org.

☐ The more at ease you feel during the viva, the better placed you'll be to confidently respond to questions. Take notes throughout; slow yourself down with deep breaths; repeat parts of your thesis when necessary; and, when in doubt over a particular question, ask the examiners for clarification.

☐ While it's natural to fear the worst, try and remove the fear of failure as a possibility in your mind. It is actually rare for a student to make it all the way to the viva stage and end up failing.

☐ Life after a PhD is a huge transition and will require some adjustment. Completing your PhD may feel like it's the end of a journey; remember that it's also the beginning of a new journey. Take time to celebrate your achievement.

CONCLUSION:
I'M A DOCTOR, WHAT COMES NEXT?

On a snowy February evening I walked up Kingsway Road in Central London. I barely noticed the hustle and bustle around me, or the extreme chill in the air. My mind was somewhere else completely. I had just passed my viva and couldn't quite believe it.

For over four years I had been telling myself 'I'll be happy when I finish my PhD.' But as much as I had day-dreamed about this moment, it didn't feel at all like I im-agined it would.

Of course, I was happy that I had made it through my PhD and also content with how the viva went. In fact, it couldn't have gone more smoothly. But something still felt slightly off.

Throughout my entire PhD experience, I recall feeling a heaviness, an immense weight on my shoulders. In darker moments, when I wasn't sure if I would ever actu-ally finish my PhD, I imagined that the viva would lift that huge weight off of me and I would finally feel free.

In many ways I did feel lighter to finally be done, but the heaviness was still there. Perhaps one of the reasons for this was because as I got nearer to my submission deadline, I had subconsciously shifted the goal posts for myself. Instead of looking to the PhD finish line as my end point, from the start of my fourth and final year of the PhD I became obsessed with the question of 'what comes next?'. I knew I had to find a job post-PhD, but had no clue what that might be. By the time I reached my viva I still wasn't sure what would come next. Despite success-fully passing my viva, there was still a heavy weight on my shoulders.

Eventually, the question of what comes next was resolved. After applying for a number of academic posts, I received an offer to start a postdoc at Oxford University. This was truly a dream come true for me. I had first visited the 'City of Dreaming Spires' when I was 19 years old and had fallen in love with it. I was delighted at the prospect of living and working in a placed steeped in so much history. After years of hard work, I could finally allow myself to take a deep breath and be happy.

Regrettably, this did not happen. No sooner had I got settled in my dream job when the goal posts shifted again. The next question I began to ask myself was 'when am I going to publish my thesis as a book?'. The pressure of trying to publish my thesis alongside the research I was conducting in Oxford became unsustainable. I felt even more stressed out than I did during my doctorate, so much so that I started to long for the days when I was a PhD student.

I could no longer deny that I was stuck on a never-ending treadmill of stress. No matter how hard I worked or how much I achieved, there would always be something else to strive for. After publishing my first book, I could already see the next thing on the horizon would be trying to secure more research funding in order to extend my postdoc.

I began to understand that the stress I was experiencing during my PhD – and now in my postdoc – didn't actually come from these external things. It came from me and how I was relating to my work – or more specifically, the perception that I needed to reach certain professional benchmarks in order to be happy. 'I'll be happy when...' started to become my default setting and, if I wasn't careful, it would be my modus operandi for life.

The thing about an 'I'll be happy when...' mindset is that by equating happiness to something outside of yourself, you end up postponing your happiness altogether. There will always be something else to achieve, and so the irony of 'I'll be happy when' is that happiness never actually arrives. And if it does, it can only be very fleeting.

It is, of course, important to keep looking ahead and working towards the next big goal. However, the danger in exclusively looking ahead is that it shifts our perspective to a point where we can easily lose sight of where we've come from and how much progress we've made.

It is no accident that I started this book off with the anecdote about my staff ID card that was issued with the wrong photo. Looking at that old photo of myself forced me to go back to the beginning of my PhD journey and really reflect on what that time was like for me. This offered me a whole new perspective. I had gotten so caught up in the everyday stresses of academic life that I started to take my journey and the milestones I had achieved along the way for granted. Recalling my past experience through the window of that photo allowed me to really appreciate – perhaps for the first time – how far I had come.

As your own PhD journey winds down, you'll naturally be inclined to look ahead at what comes next. As you do, try not to lose sight of what an incredible achievement it is to complete your doctorate. Take a moment to look back to who you were at the beginning of your journey and allow yourself to celebrate how far you've travelled.

APPENDIX:
DOCTORAL DE-STRESS
BOOK BONUSES

Visit the *AcademEase* Website (www.academease.org) to download the *Doctoral De-Stress* Book Bonuses:

BOOK BONUS 1:	Exercise: Turning Down the Volume of Your Inner Critic
BOOK BONUS 2:	Daily Work Cycle: Tips for Each Phase
BOOK BONUS 3:	Top Tips for Enhancing Your Relationship with Your Supervisor
BOOK BONUS 4:	Action Steps for Alleviating Presentation Anxiety
BOOK BONUS 5:	Tips for Navigating an Academic Q&A Session
BOOK BONUS 6:	Viva Prep Checklist

ENDNOTES

[1] Samira Shackle, 'The way universities are run is making us ill: inside the student mental health crisis' *The Guardian,* 27 September 2019, available at www.theguardian.com/society/2019/sep/27/anxiety-mental-breakdowns-depression-uk-students (accessed 11 August 2020).

[2] Visit the *AcademEase* website at www.academease.org

[3] Gill Corkindale, 'Overcoming Imposter Syndrome' *Harvard Business Review,* 7 May 2008, available at www.hbr.org/2008/05/overcoming-imposter-syndrome (accessed 11 August 2020).

[4] 'Michelle Obama: "I still have Imposter Syndrome"' *BBC News,* 4 December 2018, available at www.bbc.co.uk/news/uk-46434147 (accessed 11 August 2020).

[5] Marianne Etherson and Martin M Smith, 'How perfectionism can lead to depression among students' *The Conversation,* available at www.theconversation.com/how-perfectionism-can-lead-to-depression-in-students-97719 (accessed 11 August 2020).

[6] See https://francescocirillo.com/pages/pomodoro-technique (accessed 11 August 2020).

[7] Emilie Le Beau Lucchesi, The Unbearable Heaviness of Clutter' *New York Times,* 3 January 2019, available at www.nytimes.com/2019/01/03/well/mind/clutter-stress-procrastination-psychology.html (accessed 16 August 2020).

[8] Catherine A Roster et.al., 'The dark side of home: Assessing possession "clutter" on subjective wellbeing' *Journal of Environmental Psychology*, 46 (2016): 32-41.

[9] Download the forest app by visiting www.forestapp.cc (accessed 16 August 2020).

[10] Glenn Croston, 'The Thing We Fear More Than Death' *Psychology Today*, 29 November 2012, available at www.psychologytoday.com/gb/blog/the-real-story-risk/201211/the-thing-we-fear-more-death (accessed 11 August 2020).

[11] 'Understanding the stress response' *Harvard Health Publishing: Harvard Medical School,* 6 July 2020, available at www.health.harvard.edu/staying-healthy/understanding-the-stress-response (accessed 11 August 2020).

[12] Edwina Shaw 'How to Make Friends with Your Reptilian Brain', 31 January 2017, available at www.iahe.com/docs/articles/how-to-make-friends-with-your-reptilian-brain.pdf (accessed 11 August 2020).

Printed in Great Britain
by Amazon